THE TRUE PRIEST

Nihil Obstat: James McGrath
            Censor Librorum
Imprimatur: John Cardinal Krol
            Archbishop of Philadelphia

Verus Sacerdos was published in Italian in 1965 by Editrice Esperienze. It was originally translated into English by Arthur Gibson in 1967 and published in 1968.

In 1986, with the kind permission of the copyright holders, Gibson's English translation, especially the quotes from Saint Augustine, was revised by Audrey Fellowes.

Library of Congress Catalog Card Number: 87-71970
ISBN: 0-941491-08-0

AUGUSTINIAN PRESS
P.O. Box 476
Villanova, PA 19085

The True Priest

The Priesthood as Preached and Practiced
by Saint Augustine

by

Cardinal Michele Pellegrino

edited by

John E. Rotelle, O.S.A.

AUGUSTINIAN PRESS
1988

Contents

Augustine washes the feet of the Pilgrim Christ. Bruges Collection (1666-1668).
Artist: Érasme Quellin and Jean Érasme Quellin, disciples of Rubens.

Foreword

Cardinal Michele Pellegrino is no longer a stranger to the English-speaking world. He now has three of his books published in English: *The True Priest* was published in 1968, *Give What You Command* in 1975, and *We Are Your Servants* in 1986. In all of these books and in his many articles he shows a theological depth coupled with a deep pastoral sensitivity. However, what is more important is that the spirituality of the teacher is always an integral part in these writings.

Cardinal Pellegrino, who died on 10 October 1986, had always cultivated a deep affection for the Fathers of the Church and in particular for Saint Augustine. He knew the Fathers well, and he tried to show the world that their message is perennial. The eminent scholar penetrates well and accurately the thought of Augustine and with texts from his writings shows Augustine's rich message for today's world.

The message of Augustine on priesthood is summed up in the word "service." For Augustine this was the true meaning of ordination — service to God in transmitting the message of Jesus to humanity and service to the People of God in helping the power of God's Spirit to enter their lives. For Augustine all else is secondary, and he brings this out most clearly in his sermons to the people when he talks about his own service to them.

In Augustinian art this notion of Augustine and his ministry of service was depicted time and time again by the illustration of the "Washing of the Feet." Augustine, kneeling, washes the feet of a person who is the Pilgrim Christ, that is, Christ as he is present in men and women of all generations. The artists convey well Augustine's notion of service in this illustration, for Augustine says that in washing each other's feet we are serving Christ.

It is interesting that the task of revising and reprinting the English translation of *Verus Sacerdos,* as the book was called in its Italian original, reverts to me. In 1965, the year of my ordination to the priesthood, this book nourished my early priestly ministry. In 1966 Cardinal Pellegrino, who from time to time visited Collegio Santa Monica in Rome, suggested that an English translation be made when he discovered how enthused we were about the book. Unfortunately, due to other work, no one there could take on the task. However, we were happy to hear some years later that *Verus Sacerdos* had appeared in English.

The book was printed in England by the Society of Saint Paul and placed under the copyright of Palm Publishers. It was translated by Arthur Gibson. In 1975 I tried to secure copies of the English edition and discovered that it was out of print. It took me some time to find the copyright owner to inquire about reprinting the book.

In the meantime, I secured permission from Cardinal Michele Pellegrino to translate the book into English, for I was convinced that I would not be able to ascertain the copyright holders. It was at this time that I discovered that Philosophical Library of New York held the copyright on the English translation.

Since the company was not interested in reprinting the book, Mrs. Rose Morse Runes, the director, graciously allowed me to print it and also, at my request, to retouch the English translation, especially the passages from Saint Augustine which I felt needed some recasting.

It is my pleasure to present once again to the English-speaking world this masterpiece on the priesthood as preached and practiced by Saint Augustine of Hippo. It is my hope that this reprinting will enable present and future generations of priests to nourish their priestly commitment on the thought of Saint Augustine and present and future generations of all believers to capture the notion of service preached by Christ and so well grasped by Saint Augustine in his life and in his writings.

13 November 1987   John E. Rotelle, O.S.A.
Birth of Augustine of Hippo

Introduction

In this little book I have collected several articles, published between 1962 and 1965, in the review *Seminarium,* published by the Sacred Congregation of Seminaries and Universities, which I thank for its kind permission to reprint the articles here.

It has been my hope that this publication might make available to a great number of my fellow priests the doctrine and example of Saint Augustine, for their enlightenment and encouragement. I have been strengthened in this hope by the opinions of those whose authority and competence I respect. I am persuaded, as I believe are all who have seriously dipped into his writings, that Saint Augustine's thought and writings have not lost their power or their topicality. The priest of the twentieth century can draw valuable guidance and instruction from Augustine. Of course, the guidelines must be interpreted and adapted with a real sensitivity to the crying needs of the world in which our own ministry is exercised.

We have here attempted, not a thorough critical study of the various problems connected with our topic, but rather an entirely practically oriented exposition. We have preferred ample citations from the original Augustinian texts to any protracted personal examination.

The reader will find repetitions, both in the citations of Augustinian texts and in the commentary upon these texts. This is understandable in a series of articles composed over a period of four years. But it is equally obvious that we could have reworked the articles to eliminate all such repetition in them, when we were preparing them for publication in this little volume. We have refrained from doing so because we considered certain texts well worth repeating and certain themes well deserving of recurrent treatment.

When I was compiling these articles for publication in their present form, my first intention had been to dedicate them in the first instance to the priests and seminarians, the pastors and seminary professors of the Fossano diocese, who had been the respected associates and companions of my forty years of priestly life since my ordination on 19 September 1925. To them and to all the great company of well-loved Christians of Fossano, I intended to make a present of this little book, as a token of my esteem and affection.

But the circle has been greatly widened, beyond all possible expectation, by a recent event that has given a new direction to my own activities. Called by Christ's Vicar on earth to govern the Archdiocese of Turin, I have decided to dedicate this little book to all my brothers and sisters in Christ in this Archdiocese. May this modest tribute be at once a sign of Christian affection and a blueprint of the program of Christian activity we are committed to implement, bishop, clergy, and faithful in generous collaboration, with the grace of Christ impelling and assisting us.

May Augustine's picture of *the true priest* serve as inspiration for our daily effort to respond to our common vocation, humbly and unselfishly, from the deep wellsprings of an enlightened inner life, in brotherly love and apostolic enthusiasm.

This little gift is for all of them; my elder brothers in Christ's priesthood, full of years and merit; those now at the height of their powers and generous in their labors for God's kingdom; the new recruits who invigorate us and spur us on with their youthful enthusiasm; and the seminarians who are on the point of becoming fellow workers in our ranks.

It is my hope and my desire that these pages shall reach every priest of the church in Turin, including those few whom we have not the joy of seeing near us or of meeting in our visitations, because of painful happenings, whose inner meaning is known to God alone, that have led them away from the priestly family. I want them to know that they are numbered among those who are dearest to the heart of their Archbishop.

May Christ Jesus, the one and only everlasting mediator, who has imprinted upon our souls the character of his priesthood, grant to all the priests of the Church in Turin, and to the Archbishop whose "joy and crown" they are, that great favor of "growing daily in love of God and neighbor by the daily exercise of their priestly office, remaining ever loyal to the bond of priestly fellowship, abounding in every spiritual good and bearing a lively witness to God among their fellows, emulating those priests" (and here we recall and invoke especially the saints who have shone forth from the ranks of the clergy of Turin) "who in the course of the centuries have lived often in lowly and hidden service and have left behind a shining example of holiness" (Constitution on the Church, *Lumen Gentium,* Chapter 5, 41).

Rome, 21 September 1965   + Michele Pellegrino,
Feast of Saint Matthew the Apostle   Archbishop-Elect

Saint Augustine ordained a priest by Bishop Valerius. Ottaviano Nelli (1375-1444/50), Church of Saint Augustine, Gubbio, Italy.

1

Augustine, the New Priest

HOW DID SAINT AUGUSTINE become a priest? What were his feelings at the moment of his ordination? What was his attitude toward the new life then beginning for him?

We have good documentation for a reply to all these questions: texts of Augustine himself and Possidius' biography. The questions themselves are not prompted by idle curiosity or merely academic interest. They come from a desire to get to know, at closer range, one of the most outstanding personalities ever to arise in the history of the Church; they are calculated to throw light on an important chapter in the history of the spiritual life, from which we can, even today, draw useful lessons.

We shall first give an account of the facts as they emerge from the sources. Then we shall attempt to isolate from those same sources the elements indicative of Augustine's vision of the priesthood at the moment when he realized that God was summoning him to this vocation.

Our chief sources are two sermons (355 and 356) Augustine preached near the end of his life. The two sermons have the common title, *De moribus clericorum* (The Conduct of the Clergy), or *De vita et moribus clericorum suorum* (The Way of Life and Conduct of the Clergy). They have become an integral part of the Church's official norms for priestly life, having been referred to by several councils.

The first was preached by Augustine as bishop of Hippo on 18 December 425; the second was delivered on 6 January 426. Augustine himself tells us, at the end of Sermon 355, that he was at the time feeling old beyond his years (and he was already 71); for some time he had been in failing health and he felt compelled to give the faithful a detailed report of what was happening in the bishop's house, where he and his fellow clerics were sharing a common life.

Sermon 355 had as its immediate occasion an occurrence that had disturbed the community of clergy and faithful in Hippo. Januarius, a priest who had renounced all worldly goods on entering Augustine's community, had made a will in favor of the Church just before his death. This proved him to have kept back at least something of his own, in violation of the first rule of the house forbidding any sort of personal ownership. Bishop Augustine lashes out at this defalcation (for it amounted to this in his eyes) and proceeds to give his reasons for having refused to accept Januarius' inheritance. This leads the bishop to recount how he himself came to Hippo and initiated the way of life which he is going to explain in his two sermons.

I, whom you see here as your bishop by God's gracious decree, came to this city as a young man, as many of you know. [*In fact, Augustine would have been 36 at the time, for he came to Hippo in the early part of 391.*] I was looking for a place to found a monastery in which to live together with my brothers. I had thoroughly renounced all worldly ambition: I could have amounted to something in the world but I did not want to; what I am, I did not seek to be. *Merely to stand on the steps of God's house is better than living with the wicked* (Psalm 84:11). I did not go apart from those that love the world to vie with those that hold rule over the people. At the banquet table of my Lord, I took not the place of honor but the lowest and humblest seat; and it has pleased him to say to me: *Move up higher* (Luke 14:10). I made a practice of never going to any place where I knew the episcopal see to be vacant, since my knowledge that I enjoyed a certain reputation among the servants of God made me mortally afraid of being made a bishop. I kept my guard up and did everything I could to save myself by lying low, rather than expose myself to danger by flying high. But, as I have said, the servant ought not to gainsay the master. I came to this city to see a friend I hoped to win for God by persuading him to enter our monastery.

Possidius (*Life* 3) will later explain, doubtless reporting details Augustine had given him in personal conversation, that this friend was a highly placed imperial official, an *agens in rebus*, a good-living and God-fearing Christian, who had expressed a desire to meet Augustine and had given some indication that he would follow him into the ascetic life. Possidius adds that Augustine had several meetings with this man in Hippo, but without succeeding at that time in persuading him to abandon the world.

Augustine continues: "I felt quite safe since the bishop was in good shape. But I was taken by surprise and made a priest. And this proved to be a stepping-stone to the episcopate."

Here again, Possidius (*Life* 4) fortunately fills in for us several details omitted by Augustine. The bishop of Hippo at that time was Valerius, a Greek by birth and unhappy about the fact that he was not as fluent in Latin as he felt he ought to be for the ministry of preaching. He was already an old man. Augustine, shortly after his own ordination, calls him *senex* (Letter 21, 5-6). In the course of a religious ceremony, Valerius was telling the people how badly he needed a priest and inviting them to help him find one. Augustine was present, hidden in the midst of the crowd. But someone recognized him. This man was already familiar with the life Augustine was living in Thagaste, at the head of a little community devoted to study and prayer; he also knew Augustine's published writings. He therefore proposed Augustine as the best-fitted to fill the position. The crowd enthusiastically agreed: "They laid hold of him and, as was the custom in such cases, presented him to the bishop for ordination, all crying loudly and zealously that so it should be done."

"Violence was done to me," protests Augustine, "but I must have merited it by my sins, seeing that I can find no other explanation" (Letter 21, 1).

As Possidius' parenthetical remark clearly indicates, this sort of procedure was by no means entirely unusual. The same sort of thing happened to Saint Paulinus of Nola, to Saint Jerome's brother Paulinianus and to the saint's friend Nepotianus, to the Manichean Fermus, later converted by Augustine — to cite but a few instances that happened about this same time. Augustine himself, writing in 419, seems to consider it quite normal for clerics to enter the priestly ministry and assume the obligation of celibacy under constraint from the "violence of the people" (*Adulterous Marriages* 2, 20, 22).

The noisy enthusiasm of the assembled company of Christians was in sharp contrast to the bitter weeping of Augustine himself. As the saint informs us (Letter 21, 2), some of the brethren did not understand aright the reason for his tears and tried to console him with well-meaning sympathy and encouragement which merely made matters worse. Actually a curious and somewhat amusing misunderstanding had occurred, as Possidius dryly explains, telling us explicitly that he is reporting Augustine's own comments:

> Some attributed his tears to pride and showed that they wished to console him, saying that, although of course he deserved better than the simple priesthood, nevertheless it was at least a stepping-stone to the episcopate. The man of God was, however, as he later informed us, reckoning by higher standards. And he continued to groan. He was foreseeing the dangers that would be brought upon his own life by the direction and ministry of the Church; this was the reason for his tears.

But what good could the tears of the nominee do in the face of the declared will of an assembly in uproar under the sympathetic eye of a bishop who must certainly have known something already about this man so unexpectedly sent him by providence? And Possidius concludes: "But in the end they got their way." Indeed, Augustine himself bowed to the will of the Lord whom "the servant ought not to gainsay." What else could be expected of a man accustomed to discern providential interventions in everyday life just as much as in the crucial events of history (the Augustine of the *Confessions* and the *City of God*)?

We can now isolate three main elements of Augustine's view of the priesthood and his attitude toward it.

HE DID NOT ASPIRE TO BECOME A PRIEST

The first point is the most obvious: he did not aspire to become a priest. Neither the texts we have here examined nor any other source gives the slightest indication of any attraction on Augustine's part toward the priestly office. Augustine the rhetorician had tired of his life of senseless bustle even before his final conversion (*Confessions* 6, 14, 24); and the vague ideal of the life of a philosopher had set, after his return to Africa, into a firm purpose of asceticism, involving the renunciation of his modest holdings (*Life* 3, 1) and the choice and practice of a life of prayer and study in common with a group of friends who shared his ideals. Even in that earlier period, he had been prodigal of his powers in the service of religion, writing apologetic and polemical works and drafting plans for that encyclopedia of the liberal arts, of which only the *De Musica* (Music) has survived.

Augustine was later to confide to a correspondent that, after the first six books of *Music* had been finished, he was planning to compose still more, perhaps another six, which would have treated of *melos* (melody) as the first six had treated of rhythm: "But after the weight of the ministry of the Church was imposed upon me, all these delightful occupations slipped through my fingers; and now I can scarcely even lay my hands on the manuscript" (Letter 101, 3).

There seem to have been two main reasons for his diffidence on the score of the priesthood: the contemplative life held and always would hold a captivating attraction for him; and the shortcomings he had seen in pastors with whom he had had occasion to come into closer contact gave him a healthy dread of such responsibilities. At least we would be led to suspect this second reason from certain references in Letter 21, 1-2. It was the force of circumstances that showed him the will of the Lord, which he realized he could not resist.

SERVICE OF THE CHURCH

For Augustine, as for the fathers in general, the priesthood is essentially a social office, consecrating its holder to the service of the Church. This was his view of that office which he neither desired nor expected but to which he devoted all his time and all his energies, from the moment of his ordination.

There is a curious silence in Augustine's writings, both in the first years of his priestly life and even later, concerning his specifically priestly attitude to his priestly office. There is nothing to suggest any new dimension, different from that of his religious feelings as a simple Christian. He gives no indication of seeing in a new light, as priest, his relation to the eternal priest, especially in the celebration of the eucharistic sacrifice. This silence on a point on which every priest today is urged to meditate by a long and venerable tradition is all the more surprising precisely in Augustine, who never concealed his feelings nor trammeled their expression, who spoke openly of his bitter weeping in the incident reported above, who achieved a legendary self-revelation, penetrating even to the most intimate details of the religious life, on many a page of his writings, primarily the *Confessions*.

Yet there is ample evidence of Augustine's conviction that the priesthood was a social office with stringent obligations to the community. And here he is entirely in accord with the tradition of the fathers. Certain of the fathers did not indeed emphasize the new personal relation of the priest to Christ; many highlighted their attitude of adoration, tinged with awe, toward the eucharistic mystery. But all agreed in featuring, in their notion of the priesthood, the dimension of total dedication to the Church, in a service imposed by the will of God and inspired by supernatural love.

The community of the faithful, in union with the bishop, certainly did, in those days, play a very important role in the selection of its own sacerdotal ministers, as happened in the case of Augustine himself. And this undoubtedly exerted some influence on this predominantly social conception of the priesthood, at least to the extent of determining or highlighting certain aspects of the attitude. But the chief source of this view, on the part of the fathers of the Church, is to be sought in the words of Christ himself, both in those texts (several of which we shall be examining in the further course of this study) which explicitly present the office of the priest in this light, and in those texts which stress the absolutely central place occupied in the economy of salvation by the Church, whose minister the priest is.

The priest's dedication to the Church tolerates no limitations or compromises. This is well brought out in Augustine's renunciation of all worldly cultural pursuits, as reported in Letter 101, cited above. And we might also here mention Augustine's reply to a young pagan, Dioscorus, who had somewhat haughtily and smugly asked the bishop to resolve for him a series of questions suggested by the reading of Cicero. It is unthinkable, retorts Augustine, that a bishop, weighed down as he is with all his labors for the Church, should allow himself to become involved in explanations of the Ciceronian dialogues. And if Augustine does, in fact, write to the young questioner at some length, it is only to put the whole conversation on an apologetic footing, deliberately leaving aside the purely literary and cultural aspects of the questions involved (Letter 118).

Augustine's attitude on this whole point is worth emphasizing. For him, the call to the priesthood removes the candidate from all worldly occupations, even those commonly held to be the noblest, such as the liberal arts; the priest is ineluctably and exclusively consecrated to the service of the Church by the exercise of the functions proper to the sacred ministry. Augustine would certainly not have agreed with those who boast loudly of the illustrious contributions made by priests and bishops of various eras to the arts and sciences, when theological studies and the care of souls may well have been badly neglected.

UNSHAKABLE TRUST AND CONFIDENCE

Augustine sees the priest as being furnished with an un-shakable trust and confidence from a strange source. This source is precisely that objective vision of the priestly life that pushes the human personality of the bearer of this awful dignity into the background, inasmuch as he is but the instrument chosen by Christ for the service of his Church. The priest knows himself to have been installed by God in that office of which he will one day have to render an account to God: for the priest knows that he has not been motivated by any merely personal impulse, not even the loftiest or noblest; rather he has been chosen by God for the fulfillment of the most necessary of offices that can be entrusted to a man for the good of his fellow human beings. He counts on the grace of Christ, the One Great Shepherd, who has called him to be the visible representative of that Shepherd among the sheep of his flock — "I, whom you see here as your bishop by God's gracious decree." These words are far more than a mere conventional turn of phrase; they express Augustine's calm certainty that it is God who has called him to guide the people of Hippo, first as priest and later as bishop. They exhibit a poignant tenderness toward those souls that Christ has entrusted to Augustine. They reveal a trusting abandonment to that God, who is all-powerful and all-good, who will bear Augustine up in the workaday round of duties and lighten the burden of his fearful responsibility.

2

Preparation for the Ministry

IN THE PREVIOUS CHAPTER we touched on one of Augustine's letters which provided us with some information on how he was called to the priesthood. To this, Letter 21, we must now return as to one of the most biographically informative of all Augustine's letters, in order to discover how the newly-ordained Augustine looked upon his incipient ministry and how he intended to prepare himself against the fearful responsibilities inherent in that ministry.

PREPARATION FOR MINISTRY

Augustine wrote this letter to his own bishop, Valerius, to beg for a preparatory breathing-space. He beseeches the bishop not to assign him to parish work at once, but rather to allow him a few months of freedom (apparently from the beginning of the year till Easter) so that he may prepare himself, far from Hippo, by study and prayer for his ministry.

We learn from the letter itself that Augustine had already entrusted certain of the faithful with the oral presentation of this request to the bishop, but either no reply had be forthcoming or at least not the one Augustine wanted. As a result, Augustine decides to have recourse to a written communication, as permitting him to explain his case more exhaustively and more insistently. This is our good fortune, for it has given us a detailed account of Augustine's frame of mind at the moment at which a new life was beginning for him, as a result of an event of inestimable importance for the history of the Church.

The letter opens with a remark combining healthy realism
with deep faith, as Augustine presents two opposing notions of
the priestly life:

> First of all, I beg you, in your wisdom and piety, to be
> good enough to direct your attention to this point. In this
> life, and especially in these times, there is nothing more
> comfortable, more pleasing, more coveted, than the office
> of bishop, or priest, or deacon, when it is going to be
> discharged frivously amid the plaudits of the sycophants,
> but nothing is more miserable, more dismal, more blame-
> worthy in the eyes of God. By the same token, in this life,
> and especially in these times, there is nothing more taxing,
> more arduous, more hazardous, but at the same time no
> greater happiness, in the eyes of God, than the office of
> bishop, or priest, or deacon, provided this service is
> rendered in line with the order of our King.

Thus Augustine rejects both the worldly notion of the priesthood as a career and a way to satisfy petty personal ambitions;
and, likewise, the pessimistic notion of the priesthood as full of
nothing but burdens and perils. It is a gift that can make any
man happy who exercises it in line with God's plan.

Yet Augustine does not include himself on the score of the
difficulties and responsibilities the priest must face up to. He
writes of these in no merely theoretical vein but with a
touching humility and sincerity; and we believe that many a
priest will be able, from personal experience, to understand
Augustine's attitude on this point.

He says he had never had any proper and intensive basic
training in the service of the King of Heaven; and scarcely had
he begun to grasp the rudiments of that service when he had
been forced into accepting the post of steersman's deputy, and
him barely able to manage an oar. Then he adds:

> But I think indeed that the Lord willed to chastise me in
> this way for having dared, landlubber that I was, to reprove
> the shortcomings of many a steersman, as if I were most
> knowledgeable and abler than they. In this way, when I was
> tossed onto the high seas, I began to realize how rash had
> been my criticisms (although even before that I had been
> aware of the grave perils of this ministry).

That, says Augustine, was the reason for his bitter tears on the occasion of his ordination.

Then he proceeds, with his accustomed objectivity, to resolve the apparent contradiction, and he specifies:

> Not that I had seen new waves or tempests I had not been aware of before; but the point was that I had not realized what nimble diligence was needed to steer clear of them or to brave them. I did not know my own powers and held them to be considerable. But the Lord decided to make sport of me and to show me, in the light of hard facts, just what manner of man I really was.

Seen from the outside, the priestly mission had seemed to Augustine both taxing and risky, but not beyond his own powers or capacities, and so he had allowed himself to criticize those shepherds of souls who seemed to him ill prepared for their task. Suddenly and unexpectedly faced with the responsibility himself, he felt that he could put no reliance on his own powers. But he did not give way to temptations to despair: while readily admitting that he had been punished for his own sins by what had happened, he was nonetheless convinced that God had acted out of pity for him and not to damn him. But he felt that he must, at all costs, prepare himself properly.

PROGRAM OF PRIESTLY LIFE

How, then, was he to prepare himself properly? The reply is significant as providing at least a summary outline of the whole program of the priestly life as Augustine saw it, with an insistent emphasis on the first, essential duty of the priest, the source and ground of his whole ministry.

And what is this duty? Augustine's definition of it in these first days of his priesthood is none the less eloquent for being uttered almost in parentheses: the priest is "a man . . . who administers to the people the mystery and the word of God." The same phrase recurs in a letter Augustine wrote when he was 75 to Bishop Honoratus of Thiabe, who had asked whether the clergy ought to flee before the perils of the Vandal invasion or stay and face them: "So let the servants of Christ, the ministers of his word and mystery, do what he commands or permits" (Letter 228, 2). And we find the phrase again in Possidius' account of what Augustine reported to him concerning the last days of Saint Ambrose:

> When that venerable man was lying on his deathbed, some of the faithful of high station who were standing at his bedside were saddened, as they saw that he was on the point of passing from this world to God, at the thought that the Church should be deprived of a bishop of such stature to dispense to them the word and the mystery of God; and in tears they besought him to beg of the Lord to prolong his life (*Life* 27, 7).

PRAYER AND THE STUDY OF SCRIPTURE

Augustine holds two things to be vital in the preparation for such a ministry: prayer and the study of holy Scripture; or, better and more accurately, the meditation on the word of God, accompanied by ardent prayer that he might penetrate its mystery and communicate it to the people.

Augustine sees himself as a sick man: "Knowing my infirmity, I must seek in the Scriptures the medicine for all my ills; by praying and studying (orando ac legendo), I must see to gaining for my soul the health and the strength to face such dangerous duties." Just at the moment when he was called to the priesthood, Augustine continues, he had been considering how he could find time to devote himself to the study of Scripture, not fully realizing at that time just how necessary it was going to be. "I would indeed make bold to say," he adds, "that I know and hold with candid faith the truths needful to salvation. But how am I to communicate them so as to insure the salvation of others, *without considering my own advantage but their advantage, that if possible they may be saved* (1 Corinthians 10:33)."

Augustine is well aware that the knowledge of the things of God necessary to the Christian for his own personal life is one thing, even if that Christian be dedicated to an ideal of perfection such as he had been pursuing for three years at Thagaste; and the knowledge required of him who is supposed to instruct and nurture the faithful is quite another.

> There may be — indeed there certainly are — written in the holy books counsels that the man of God (biblical expression often used by Augustine to designate the priest) must know thoroughly so as to exercise faithfully and fruitfully the ministry of the Church and, set down in the midst of sinners though he may be, to live with a clear conscience or to die in such a way as not to lose that life to which aspire the meek and humble hearts of Christians. But how can he get to know these counsels, except as the Lord has told us: by asking, seeking, knocking (Matthew 7:7; Luke 11:9), that is, by prayer, by study, by tearful supplication (*Life* 2).

Augustine is clearly aware that it is not going to be easy to extract from the bishop the favor he is so insistently asking. We must not forget that Valerius had been impelled to seek the assistance of a priest — Possidius is quite specific on this point (*Life* 2) — mainly because he felt the urgent need of having someone to take the whole load of preaching, or at least some of it, off his shoulders, since the good bishop felt himself less than adequate to this burden, what with his Greek background and ancestry, with its consequent language problem, and his advanced age. Now the period of leave Augustine was requesting covered the whole of Lent, the very time when a special intensification of the ministry of the word was called for, in order to prepare the faithful for Easter and to instruct the catechumens being prepared for baptism. In this connection, it is not without significance that Augustine, while insisting that he be granted "the full period of time I have asked for," should yet hold out the hope that he might be able "to make do with a briefer period of time than I have requested": the implication is that he might be able to come to the bishop's assistance in the days immediately preceding Easter, when the need would be greatest.

Moreover, Augustine saw an obstacle in the very esteem in which the bishop held him. Valerius judged the new priest to be fully fit for the exercise of the priestly ministry, whereas

Augustine himself, with his better and deeper knowledge of himself, was convinced he could not face it without a more searching preparation.

It is quite in character that the ex-rhetorician Augustine should here put into the mouth of the Lord himself, speaking from his high tribunal, a rebuke that was calculated to put the fear of divine judgment into the heart of the bishop as well! Imagine me, says Augustine, trying to excuse myself before God's high court by saying that I simply had not had time for the proper training because I had been busy from the outset in the practical ministry. And here is the Lord's reply as Augustine reports it:

> You wicked servant, had someone attempted to cheat the Church out of a farm cultivated assiduously for its yield of produce, you would have neglected the field that I have watered with my blood [the souls of the faithful] and would have grasped at the slightest chance of getting through to the earthly judge; and everybody would have approved, indeed some would even have laid stern injunctions upon you and constrained you to do it. And if the judgment had gone against you, you would even have crossed the sea [to appeal to the imperial tribunal]. This would have kept you away a whole year and perhaps even longer; and nobody would have complained about your absence. And all this so as not to allow others to retain possession of a holding needed not for the souls but for the bodies of the poor. And yet their hunger would be stilled in a way much easier and more pleasing to me by my own live plants, provided these plants were diligently cultivated [that is the faithful, properly instructed and exhorted, would have made up, by their charitable donations, for the deficit of funds]. Why, then, do you allege in your favor the lack of time to learn how to cultivate my field?

Then Augustine addresses himself directly to the bishop:

> Tell me, I pray you, what should my answer be? Would you really want to say: "Valerius, that good old man, believed me fully ready and was too fond of me; so he did not allow me to learn these things"?

We do not know what was the bishop's reply to this request, so urgently presented "in the name of Christ's goodness and his sternness, of his mercy and his judgment," and in the name of the affection the venerable old bishop had shown to the young priest in word and deed. But Augustine's letter itself is of capital importance for our understanding of the frame of mind in which he entered on his ministry. That is why we have reported it in such detail.

The comparison between the field watered by the blood of Christ and the farm considered worth the expenditure of time and energies is eloquent of Augustine's unbending persuasion that the priest's assignment was a spiritual one. This is the Augustine who always lived in voluntary poverty, in Thagaste and at Hippo alike, as layman, as priest, and as bishop, in community with his like-minded brothers who had, like him, renounced all personal property (Sermon 355, 2; *Life* 24, 13); this is the Augustine who braved the criticism of many to refuse endowments made to the Church in Hippo when others considered that such endowments had injured their rights (Sermon 355, 4) or when an acceptance of the endowments would have involved the Church in financial responsibilities or lawsuits (Sermon 355, 5). This is the Augustine who staged no personal mammoth building campaigns, though he did not object to others staging such campaigns in moderation (*Life* 24, 13); who did not attend personally to the administration of the goods of Church and presbytery, both of which were looked after by clerics delegated by him (*Life* 24, 1); who was only impelled by the duty of charity and the consideration of the good of souls to spend any time on occupations not strictly pertinent to his ecclesiastical ministry, such as court sessions (*Life* 19, 1-5) and business visits or correspondence with the civil authorities (*Life* 19, 6); who imitated Mary rather than Martha in shaking off these burdens as soon as possible to devote himself to prayer, to study, to preaching, to the administration of the sacraments, and to the composition of those writings that were an essential part of his ministry (*Life* 24, 10-12).

To the program of the priestly life outlined in Letter 21, Augustine was to remain faithful throughout the entire forty years of his service to the Church. It was a constant struggle with himself to overcome his own personal inner tension between the craving for contemplation and the demands of an active life, often jading and oppressive. He overcame this tension by keeping eyes and heart fixed, amid the ever stronger temptations to flee to solitude, upon him who died for all, so that those who live should live not by and for themselves but for him who died for them (*Confessions* 10, 24). Christ alone is Augustine's food and drink, a nourishment that he distributes to others, even as he longs to be filled with this food and drink among those who eat of it and are filled.

3

The Ministry of the Word and the Mystery of God

NOW THAT WE HAVE TREATED of the strange providence whereby Augustine was called to the priesthood so unexpectedly and have inspected his attitude to that ministry as revealed in his famous Letter 21 to Valerius and by other writings of his early (and later) priestly days, it will be useful to cast a rapid glance over the whole of his priestly life, with a view to seeing what exactly were his activities. This we believe to be in line with the method of procedure indicated by our subtitle. Even a brief and summary review of the actual activities of Augustine, as priest and bishop, will help us better to penetrate into the soul of this servant of the Church to discover there the deep wellspring of his actions and the ideal that inspired him in the plethora of his daily activities.

We feel it to be both pointless and inappropriate, in a study that does not claim to be a biography of Augustine, to distinguish between his activity as priest (391-395) and his activity as bishop (395-430). The information Possidius (*Life* 5-7) gives us on the period of Augustine's priesthood is undoubtedly highly interesting, but it makes no real distinction between Augustine's activity as priest and that which he was to deploy for more than thirty years as bishop. Nor do we find any such clear-cut distinction in any of Augustine's own writings. Moreover, we should not forget that Bishop Valerius of Hippo had ordained Augustine as a priest primarily to have his help in a ministry, then commonly held to be proper to the bishop: the ministry of preaching.

LITURGICAL ACTIVITY

We have already cited two passages from Augustine's letters, echoed by a statement of his biographer, which show that Augustine considered the core of the priestly ministry to be "the ministry of the word and the mystery of God." The "mystery" obviously embraces the various liturgical aspects of the episcopal office: from the celebration of the eucharistic mystery to the administration of what we in the West call "sacraments" and Eastern fathers prefer to call "mysteries," preeminent among which are baptism and penance. But there must also be included in this aspect of the ministry the celebration of the great feasts, especially those of apostolic origin or those sanctioned by ecumenical councils, such as Easter, Ascension, and Pentecost (see Letter 54, 1).

It is no cause for surprise that this latter sort of liturgical activity should have left few traces in the writings of Augustine himself or of his biographer. Augustine was much more inclined to meditation on the word of God in its inner truth and meaning as inspiration of the Christian life than to any rapturous reflection on or technical tabulation of the external aspects of liturgical practice. We might instance his gingerly distrust of the psalms, where he feared lest the aesthetic delight engendered might cloud the purity of the inner religious sense (see *Confessions* 10, 33). Or again we might mention his reference to Psalm 45:14: *omnis pulchritudo filiae regis intrinsecus* (all the beauty of the king's daughter is within), which Augustine uses to show that the essential thing is to keep intact the unity of the faith, while external customs and practices can vary without detriment, since they touch only the outer garment of the Church, *in fimbriis aureis circumamicta varietatibus* (in borders of gold, woven about with varieties) (Letter 36, 9, 22). Or finally we might note Augustine's indifference to splendor in church buildings and liturgical offices. And it is quite understandable that Possidius should feel neither need nor inclination to lay special stress on a kind of activity wherein a bishop, in the normal course of affairs, had no chance to excel.

Yet the texts are not entirely silent in this regard. Those points we can easily conjecture from the history of liturgy in the period in question find confirmation and integral mention in several Augustinian passages.

As bishop, Augustine showed great solicitude for those who remained for many long years catechumens; he instructed and exhorted them himself. But even greater was his concern for and commitment to the competentes who were being prepared during Lent for baptism by an intensive program of instructions, exorcisms, and examinations. The fruits of this labor were harvested with the entry of the new Christians into the Church. Here too the bishop had a strenuous obligation in the shape of the solemn Easter Vigil, comprising the long scriptural readings, the chanting of the psalms, the exhortation, the profession of faith and the interrogation of the candidates, the administration of baptism and confirmation, and the celebration of the eucharist. The daily instruction of the neophytes during the Easter Octave set the seal on the rites of Christian Initiation.

But every Sunday was a little Easter. The resurrection of the Lord was to be commemorated in the liturgical assembly, presided over by the bishop, who listened to the scripture readings, explained them in the sermon, celebrated the sacrifice, and distributed communion.

Then, too, Augustine (*The Lord's Sermon on the Mount* 2, 7, 25-26) considered (in common with the fourth and fifth century fathers) that the practice of daily communion was normal and desirable, though he states that he respects divergent usages and opinions (Letter 54, 10, 4). It can therefore be readily imagined what an immense burden of work was involved for the bishop and his assistants in the administration of this sacrament.

A grave responsibility of the bishop, aided by the priests when occasion demanded, was, in Augustine's eyes, the ministry to sinners: some had to be excluded from communion and have a penance imposed by proper authority in cases of public or scandalous faults; others had to be readmitted to reconciliation after having performed the penance assigned.

In cases of public calamities, such ministrations were anxiously sought even by those who took little thought for them in normal circumstances: "What a crowd of people, then, of both sexes and of every age, streams into the church to ask one for baptism, another for reconciliation, still another for a penance, and all for a little comfort and the administration and distribution of the sacraments" (Letter 228, 8; see *Life* 30, 29).

Finally, we can mention the bishop's practice of attending the marriage ceremonies of the faithful, to seal the vows with his authoritative presence and to give husband and wife his blessing. Augustine definitely considers this to be a duty of the pastor, whereas he firmly disapproves of any priest acting as marriage broker for anybody (*Life* 27, 4-5).

PREACHING

Side by side with the administration of the sacraments and integrally interwoven into the liturgical action, Augustine placed the ministry of the word. On this aspect of his priestly activity, we have the fullest particulars. But in view of our intention to devote two whole chapters to it later, we shall here limit ourselves to just a few relevant points.

Possidius (*Life* 7, 1) uses the words of the Acts of the Apostles to describe Augustine's preaching activity from the outset of his priesthood: called by the bishop to assist him in this ministry, the presbyter Augustine "taught and preached in private and in public, in home and in church, *the message of salvation* (Acts 13:26), *fearlessly* (Acts 4:29)." And near the end of his account of this amazing life, the biographer again highlights the ministry of preaching: "Right up to the last illness, he kept preaching in the church the word of God, assiduously, zealously, courageously, outspokenly, and with all the vigor of his great mind" (*Life* 31, 4).

The actual sermons of Augustine that have come down to us are, of course, the prime sources, incomplete to be sure but of incalculable value, for the documentation of this preaching activity over the whole period of forty years between the two references just cited. Of the eleven volumes (aside from those containing indexes and studies on Augustine) devoted to the works of Saint Augustine in Migne's *Patrologia Latina*, five (XXXV-XXXIX) are entirely devoted to his sermons. One whole group of these sermons is made up of sets of consecutive commentaries on books of the Bible (John's gospel and the first letter on 1 John, and the psalms); and in addition there are about five hundred sermons on individual scriptural texts or for liturgical feasts on various special occasions.

Augustine never actually prepared his sermons in writing. He made no effort to put them into a formal style before delivering them. "Saint Augustine never wrote down nor dictated his sermons himself. After meditating, he delivered them under the inspiration of the moment. In other words, he improvised." And it is to the stenographers that we must be grateful for the fine and exhaustive texts of these sermons that have come down to us; they meticulously recorded the words of the bishop as he spoke and later made those collections of sermons to which the manuscript tradition goes back (*Life* 7, 3).

But if Augustine did no sermon writing, he certainly never stinted in the matter of sermon preaching: every Sunday, on the feast day of the martyrs, Saturday, and on the vigils of all feast days, he would invariably preach to the people. And when he was on the road, his preaching assignments were multiplied still more to satisfy the desire of the faithful. Possidius tells us;

> When he was made bishop, he preached the word of eternal salvation with still greater perseverance and ardor and with still greater authority, no longer in one region only but wherever he was asked to go; always he responded with alacrity and zeal, while the Church of the Lord grew and prospered; always he was ready to give a reason to whoever asked him, for the faith that was in him and the hope in God (*Life* 9, 1).

In Carthage, for example, in 403, he preached once on 25 August, twice on the following day, mentioning at the beginning of his second sermon that "both proclaiming and listening to the word of truth is hard work" (*Expositions on the Psalms* 32, sermon 2, 1), and then once again on 27 August.

Possidius has an interesting remark on Augustine's approach to preaching: after reporting that Augustine considered himself "to have been appointed by God as a sentry to the house of Israel (see Ezekiel 3:17; 33:7), to preach the word of God, insistently in season and out of season, refuting falsehood, correcting error, calling to obedience, teaching with the utmost patience (see 2 Timothy 4:2)," Possidius adds: "and especially did he concentrate on instructing persons who would be capable of teaching others as well" (*Life* 19, 5).

WRITING

In the passage already referred to (*Life* 7, 1), Possidius, in speaking of Augustine's preaching activity, brackets the saint's writings with his sermons as witness to his impassioned activity: "both in the form of carefully prepared books and in the form of extemporaneous discourses." And Possidius recurs to the same theme immediately afterward (*Life* 7, 3), mentioning the "books and discourses, poured out by God's wonderful grace that inspired him, solidly buttressed by cogent reasoning and the authority of the sacred Scriptures."

Possidius knew his hero's soul to its core and he was well aware that Augustine's writing activity was but one aspect, albeit undoubtedly an essential one, of the inexhaustible fervor with which the saint devoted himself to the service of the Church. The entire mass of books that he dictated and published, so many in number that "a scholar would be hard put just to read them all intelligently," all had the aim and object of either refuting heretics or procuring "the edification of the holy sons and daughters of the Church" (*Life* 18, 9).

Not a single work can be found among Augustine's writings after his ordination that is not patently religious in theme. Even after his baptism, he had indeed worked, during the very productive "leisure time" (otium) at Thagaste, on the ambitious plan of an encyclopedia of the liberal arts. It was then that he wrote the *De Musica,* in which to be sure he did speak, at least in Book VI, of the value of a study on the way "to arrive from mutable numbers at immutable numbers which are within the immutable truth itself" (*Revisions* 1, 10, 1). But the work was never completed; and the reason Augustine himself gives is that he had in the meantime shouldered "the burden of parochial work" (Letter 101, 3).

There is no question but that the new duties did take up all of the time and energies of the cleric and hierarch, making it physically impossible for him to give any time to the other studies that had for so long been his "delight" (as he himself says in that passage we have already cited). But there was a deeper motive at work here as well, imparting a strictly sacral bias to all the work of Augustine the student and the writer and inducing him to leave to one side every intellectual occupation of a worldly sort, however noble and worthy that occupation might be in itself.

Augustine's letter to the young pagan, Dioscorus, shows the bishop as firmly convinced that a bishop (or a priest for that matter), entirely consecrated as he is to the service of the Church, ought not to waste his time explaining Cicero's dialogues. In his reproof to this young gentleman for his unreasonable request, a request motivated more by personal vanity than by an sincere love of truth (Letter 118, 2-3), Augustine makes mention not only of the Church duties that give him no respite but also of the inappropriateness of a bishop becoming involved in this sort of purely secular cultural activity. And if Bishop Augustine does indeed allow himself to send the youngster a lengthy reply, taking advantage of a brief convalescence spent away from Hippo, it is simply to profit by the occasion to admonish the boy with fatherly insistence, exhorting him especially to that salutary humility that will lead him to submit to Christ and thus find the only royal road to truth (Letter 118, 21-23).

Moreover, the greater part of the writings Augustine has left us were not prompted by any spontaneous choice of a subject matter; nor were they inspired even by pastoral considerations; rather they were written at the request (often repeated and insistent) of persons who wished to be enlightened on various points of doctrine; or they arose out of the urgent demands of polemical controversy with heretics and pagans.

THE GREAT POLEMICAL WRITINGS

No bishop in Augustine's day could confine pastoral activity to the limits of the flock faithful to orthodoxy and to the unity of the Church. Both the orthodoxy of the Church in Africa and its unity were gravely threatened by heresy and schism respectively.

Manicheism, so widespread in the fourth and fifth centuries, "was then raging in epidemic proportions in the city of Hippo; many, townsmen and strangers alike, had been infected by it to the marrow of their bones" (*Life* 7, 1). No one was better qualified than Augustine to realize the peril it posed and to unmask its errors, for Augustine himself had succumbed to the seductive doctrine of Manes and had worked himself loose from it only with great difficulty.

The schism of Donatus had split Africa into two antagonistic churches, provoking, in addition to the confusion of spirits, civil disorders and violence, in a complex interplay of various political, economic, and social factors, which merely served to sharpen the already drastic religious dissension. Even as he was deepening his own sense of the economy of salvation, in his meditation on the word of God, Augustine as bishop could not make his peace with this rent in the seamless robe of Christ and he exerted himself everywhere to put the faithful on their guard and to bring back the straying sheep to the one fold.

Just when the Donatist fortunes were rapidly on the wane, thanks in great part to Augustine himself but not without the vigorous intervention of the civil authorities, just at the decisive turning point represented by the great Synod of Carthage in 411, Africa was beginning to be infiltrated with a new and insidious, written and spoken venom, the heresy of the Pelagians which undermined the very foundations of Christianity by its practical denial of the supernatural. It is Augustine's crowning merit that he grasped, from the very outset, the error lurking under the cloak of an asceticism capable of winning the new movement broad sympathies, and that the energetic bishop provided essential clarifications on the doctrines of grace and predestination, even though Augustine's trenchant enunciations in this whole domain may perhaps have needed some modifications.

Another, though considerably less dangerous heresy with which Augustine had to contend was that of the Arians. And contend he did, though to a much lesser degree than with the other heresies already mentioned, with this Arian aberration which was often quite influential because of the support it got in imperial administrative circles.

And finally, Augustine's polemical and apologetic writings and activity were directed against paganism, long since banned by repeated imperial decrees and now devoid of any deep religious or cultural vitality, but nonetheless still capable of exerting a kind of fascination on certain aristocratic circles, loyal to ancestral traditions, and on certain strata of the common people that had not yet been won over to Christianity.

Augustine's two main forms of polemical-apologetic activity, preaching and writing, were largely inspired by the desire to combat such errors and convert the victims of them. We must also here mention another modality of Augustine's fight against heresy, one specially apt to shed still further light on his own strong and multi-faceted personality and to show how this bishop conceived and fulfilled his mission. We refer to the disputations, the public debates, to which Augustine attributed a great importance, *ready,* as it is written, *to give a reason to whoever asked him for the faith that was in him and the hope in God* (1 Peter 3:15) and *capable of expounding the true doctrine and refuting those who argue against it* (Titus 1:9) and animated by the unshakable confidence he had in the final triumph of the truth: "the victory is always that of truth" (Sermon 296, 14).

Sometimes these confrontations were by public request, as on the occasion when both Catholics and Donatists in Hippo asked the priest Augustine to meet the priest Fortunatus. Defeated and routed in the encounter, Fortunatus left the city for good (*Life* 7). A disputation with another Manichean, "the elect" Felix, resulted in the conversion of this heretic (*Life* 16).

At the conference held in Carthage between the Catholic and the Donatist bishops, from 1 to 8 June 411, Augustine was officially only one of the seven representatives of the Catholic bishops, but Possidius is quite justified in speaking of the encounter as a victory of his hero (*Life* 13). Seven years later, Augustine was to try in vain to arrange a public disputation, in the Church, with Hemeritus, Donatist bishop of Caesarea in Mauritania (*Life* 14). Augustine likewise held public debates with two protagonists of Arianism, Count Pascentius and Bishop Maximinus, in the latter case, "at the desire and request of many" (*Life* 17), as Possidius informs us.

These disputations, we are told in the passages cited, were always arranged with great punctiliousness and with stenographers present to take down a word for word record. If the debating opponent obstinately refused to allow this, then Augustine took upon himself the burden of writing down a faithful report (Letter 33, 4).

EXTRA-DIOCESAN ACTIVITIES

It is already clear from what has thus far been said that "that unforgettable man, chief member of the body of the Lord, was always solicitous and most vigilant for the good of the Church universal" (*Life* 18, 6). He often had to extend his activity beyond the confines of his diocese of Hippo, not only by his writings which were begged of him by various other localities, not only by his extensive correspondence which not infrequently involved him in the answering of broad ranging and difficult questions, so that some of his letters developed into little treatises, but also by his physical presence wherever it was judged necessary for the good of the Church. ·

From the time of his return from the five year stay in Italy, Augustine never again undertook sea voyages, declaring that his infirm state of health precluded them (Letter 122, 1). But even so he was not a stay-at-home, as he would have preferred to be, so as to attend to the needs of his faithful, to prayer and to study. For he had to take part in councils held frequently in the primatial see of Carthage, and in the various provinces; then too, the disputations of which we have spoken already, the election and consecration of bishops, important affairs of various churches, all these required Augustine to travel quite frequently. An eminent scholar who has made a fine critical study of this whole point felt justified in summing up his conclusions by calling Augustine "a man continually on the road."[1]

The results of this study show that there were barely ten years, between Augustine's ordination and his death, in which he was not demonstrably absent from Hippo for some period of time, and there is no cogent argument against supposing that some of his journeys, of which we have no known date, may have fallen within these years. Sometimes Augustine made three, four, or even five journeys a year. Carthage was the destination farthest away from Hippo; and Augustine went there 25 times (as far as we can ascertain) to take part in as many councils. On such occasions, he preached frequently in Carthage. On other occasions he was called to the metropolis to preach or to attend to other duties. If we bear in mind that the distance between Hippo and Carthage varies, over the three possible routes, between 152 and 178 miles, to be traveled in daily stages of from 16 to 19 miles, rarely in a carriage, at best on horseback or mule or donkey (Augustine having perhaps been carried in a litter when he was old or sick), and that Augustine was frequently invited to preach in the

1. O. Perler, "Les voyages de Saint Augustin," in *Recherches Augustiniennes,* vol. I, Paris, 1958, page 42.

cities and towns through which he was passing, then we can get some idea of the time and energies these journeys must have cost him. We also know of one journey from Carthage to Caesarea in Mauritania, more than 600 miles (1,000 kilometers) away.

SECULAR BUSINESS

Augustine never complained of these taxing trips. It was, in his eyes, quite right and proper that a bishop should expend his time and energies for the Church. What really weighed upon him was the fact that he had to get involved in activities he deemed far from comfortable to the spiritual mission of a pastor of souls, even though necessitated by circumstances and providing yet another occasion to aid his flock.

The bishop had to spend much time on the cases that Catholics and non-Catholics alike submitted to his tribunal (the *episcopalis audientia*, recognized by civil law). Augustine devoted himself to these hearings "sometimes until the hour of luncheon, sometimes prolonging his fast the entire day." A careful and impartial judge, he aimed, in all this work, solely at "the advantage of Christian souls, paying heed to what would aid men and women to advance in the faith and in good morals and to what would make them fall away from either," and taking every occasion "to teach and instill into the litigants the truths of the law of God and to train them, putting them in mind of the means suited to the attainment of eternal life" (*Life* 19, 2-4).

Recommendations — there was a great cross often impossible to avoid. It is true that several times "when asked by persons most dear to him for letters of recommendation to the civil authorities, he did not give them" either to avoid compromising himself by vouching for the unworthy or to avoid being himself asked in turn for favors he would not have been able, in conscience, to grant. But in many cases charity compelled the bishop to intervene with a letter to the authorities; and such letters he had a knack of composing "with such dignity and discretion that, far from appearing a nuisance, they even earned him admiration." But the biographer is outspoken in remarking on how much all this sort of thing cost Augustine: "This duty, which kept him from better things, he considered a burden, always finding his pleasure rather in talking of the things of God publicly or at home, in personal conversation with his friends and brothers" (*Life* 19, 6 — 20).

Wherever there was not an overriding need for his personal intervention, he was always glad to dispense with any purely secular business. Since the laity would not permit the Church to give up those holdings that involved administrative responsibilities, Bishop Augustine entrusted the management of such holdings to his clerics who rendered him an annual account of them. He never bought real estate, never accepted trusteeships, engaged in no new building campaigns himself, though not forbidding others to launch such campaigns, within the bounds of moderation (*Life* 23-24).

Obviously Augustine had to have a impervious spirit of detachment, an invincible desire for God and the things of God, in order not to allow himself to be overwhelmed by the plethora of pastoral assignments and in order, despite it all, to find time for prayer and for the great amount of writing of which we have already spoken.

STUDY AND PRAYER

Possidius stresses, in the passage already cited: "Intent as he was on things of greater importance, that is, things spiritual, and wholly absorbed in them, it was a major maneuver for him to detach his mind, from time to time, from things eternal in order to lower it to matters temporal. And as soon as these temporal affairs had been dealt with and brought into order, his soul freed itself from them as from things prickly and irksome, to return to the inner and higher realities of the spirit, to the search for the divine truths, or to the dictation of what he had already found, or to the correction of what had already been written at his dictation. Thus did he persist, laboring the

whole day through and keeping vigil in the night watches"
(*Life* 24, 10-12). In this, continues Possidius, Augustine
resembles Mary, the sister of Martha.

Only by a heroically unwavering resolve never to lose a
single moment of time, even to the extent of stealing hours
from sleep, was Augustine able to leave behind such a mass of
writings, many of which are the fruit, not only of a vast amount
of careful reading, but also of that searching analysis and
meditation that was typical of one of the loftiest and finest
minds humanity has ever known.

Augustine did not consider himself a professional scholar:
called by God to be a pastor, he expended all his energies in
the interests of the flock entrusted to him. In 404, he writes to
Saint Jerome, telling that peppery old scripture scholar that he
intends to send some of his own pupils to the school of the
illustrious exegete, if Jerome is willing; and Augustine adds:
"since there is not nor can there ever be in me such an eminent
knowledge of the divine scriptures as I see to be in you. And
what little familiarity and experience I have in this field, I use
as best I can on behalf of the people of God. My ecclesiastical
duties absolutely preclude any more diligent attention to
studies than what is required for the instruction of the people"
(Letter 73, 5).

In presenting Augustine to us, in the passage cited above,
"as that most religiously minded Mary, figure and type of the
Church celestial, of whom it is written that *she sat at the feet of
the Lord intent on listening to his words* (Luke 10:39),"
Possidius draws our attention to the deep roots of the interior
life of Augustine of Hippo, his spirit of prayer, of contemplation,
of union with God. But even more illuminating than the
remark of the biographer is the entire corpus of Augustine's
works: from the magnificent prayer of the catechumen in the
Soliloquies (1, 1, 2-6) to the *Confessions*, in which it is prayer
that inspires and pervades the recall of the past, the reflection
on the present and the meditation on scripture, making the
work a unique masterpiece of religious literature. The whole of
his literary heritage, including those lyrical contemplative
passages to which he gives rein here and there in his letters and

sermons, is an eloquent witness to a spirit living in the bright light of faith, of that faith to which he devotes his study and his ministry.

Possidius' account of Augustine's last days on earth confirms and seals the testimony of the saint's own writings:

> He had written out for himself those psalms of David that treat of penitence, and during his illness, he would look from his bed where he was lying at those pages that had been put up on the wall opposite. He would read them and as he read the tears were always warm upon his cheeks. To prevent his recollection being disturbed by anyone whatsoever, he begged us, ten days before he departed the body, not to allow anyone to enter his room outside the hours when the doctors came to visit him or when his meals were brought to him. His wish was respected to the letter. And for all that time he devoted himself to prayer (*Life* 31, 2-3).

But this has already led us beyond the limits we had set ourselves in this chapter, an overall view of Augustine's activities as priest and bishop. Here we are beginning to catch a glimpse of the spirit that animates and explains the amazing volume of his work, destined to leave such a deep mark on the history of the Church and of the entire human race. It is this interior world that alone can render intelligible something of the priesthod as conceived and lived by Augustine. And of that we shall have to speak now in greater detail.

4

We Are the Servants of His Church

CAN WE SINGLE OUT ONE dominant note, one unifying spirit, pervading the intensive and many-sided activity Augustine engaged in throughout the forty years of his sacerdotal and episcopal ministry (of which we have just presented a summary overall account)? Is there one clue that would explain the deepest and truest meaning of such indefatigable industry?

Augustine's own words which we have chosen as title for the chapter (*The Work of Monks* 29, 37) seem to us to provide just that clue. To any question about the significance of the priesthood in Saint Augustine (as, indeed, in all the fathers), we believe the answer must be that they all see the priesthood as a social function, consecrating him who is signed with the priestly character to the unremitting service of the Church. Augustine does not give any special prominence, on the other hand, to the notion of the surpassing dignity of the priest as minister of the awful mysteries accomplished upon the altar (for example, the famous passage of Saint John Chrysostom in *On the Priesthood* III, 46), nor yet to the vision, more current in recent trends of spirituality, of the intimate mystical relation between the priest and Christ.

NOT AT THE HEAD, BUT AT THE SIDE

Augustine is certainly not unaware of the authority vested in the bishop. He asserts it on occasion and, above all, he exercises it, conscious of thereby fulfilling a specific and important duty.

The bishop commands and the faithful are bound to obey: "Just as we must reflect with great fear and anxiety on how we may fulfill the office of bishop without blame, so your own care must be to strive to be humbly obedient to all the commands given to you" (Sermon 340, 2).

Nor does Augustine hesitate, when he deems it necessary, to reprove the culprits openly, as the faithful well know:

> I think, for I speak in the presence of God, that I seek nothing from you other than your salvation, and often I groan at the sins of my fellow Christians. I am outraged and tortured in mind, and sometimes I reproach them, or rather, I never refuse to reproach them. All who remember what I say are witnesses to how many times I have reproached our sinful brothers and sisters, and reproached them severely (Sermon 137, 14).

Among those many witnesses one was undoubtedly Possidius, who was to say: "He would reprove, in the hearing of all, those who had sinned, to the end that the others should be afraid of sinning" (*Life* 19, 4), as Saint Paul advised in 1 Timothy 5:20.

But the proper exercise of this authority is precisely ordered to the rendering of a service. One of the plays on words (of which generally speaking the ex-rhetorician Augustine was all too fond!)[1] gives especially forceful expression to this notion. Excusing himself to the Proconsul Hapringius for a demarche that might appear importunate, Augustine declares that this step had been inspired by a rightful solicitude for the Church entrusted to him, for whose best interests he takes thought ("cuius utilitatibus servio"), his intention being to stand "not at the head but at the side," that is, not so much to command as rather to be of service. The original play on words "non tam praeesse quam prodesse" can only be brought out in English by recasting the construction (Letter 134, 1).

"We are chiefs and leaders," says Augustine in a sermon (340A, 3) delivered in Carthage in 412, on the occasion of the

---

1. See C. Mohrmann, "Das Wortspiel in den Augustinischen Sermone," in *Etudes sur le latin des Chrétiens,* Rome, 1958, pages 323-349.

consecration of a bishop, "and we are servants, we are at your head, but only if we are at your side (praesumus, sed si prosumus)."

And on the anniversary of his own episcopal consecration Augustine delivered this exhortation to his people: "Come to our aid with your prayers and your obedience, so that it shall be our delight to be not so much at your head as at your side (ut nos vobis non tam praeesse, quam prodesse delectet)" (Sermon 340, 1).

It is the merit of those who "mingled with the crowd, to govern souls by action and exhortation, not aiming to be at the head but to be by the side (non ut praesint, set ut prosint)," to radiate some glimmer of that wisdom that is attained in the solitary contemplation of the truth (*Answer to Faustus* 22, 56).

The man would not be truly a bishop, concludes Augustine, "who would delight in being at the head rather than at the side (qui praeesse dilexerit, non prodesse)" (*City of God*, 19, 19, 29).

The Augustinian formula so happily expressive of the gospel notion of authority was to find well-deserved fame in the tradition of the Church. Suffice it to cite here two of the greatest masters of the divine art of ruling souls. Saint Benedict admonishes the abbot as follows: "And know that it befits you better to be at the side than to be at the head (prodesse magis quam praeesse)."[2] And Saint Gregory the Great says of the pastors of the Church: "Let them take pleasure not in being at the head of men and women but rather in being at their side (nec praeesse se hominibus gaudeant, sed prodesse)."[3]

The same thought recurs elsewhere in Augustine, without the word play:

2. *Rule,* Saint Benedict, 64, 8.
3. *Pastoral Rule,* Saint Gregory the Great, 1, 6.

> Since you are given leaders (praepositi) whose duty it is to care for those they lead (consulant eis quibus praesunt), and by no means to seek their own advantage from their position as leader but that of those they serve (quibus ministrant), if any have been set over you whose aim is to rejoice in their leadership, seeking their own honor in it and considering their own interests only, they feed themselves and not their sheep (Sermon 46, 2, 41).

Moreover, we shall have occasion to see how the bishop of Hippo several times appeals to his own authority precisely in those situations in which he protests that he wants to exercise it solely in the service of the faithful and to their advantage. We shall take account, in our study of Augustine's thought on this whole problem, only of those passages in which the "serve" is understood directly of the pastoral office, leaving to one side all the many texts in which Augustine himself or those who speak of him, primarily Possidius, use the expressions *servus Dei* (servant of God) and *servire Deo* (to serve God) in a clearly ascetical sense, referring to those who have taken religious vows.

The passage we have used as title of this chapter seems to us to pinpoint best of all the sense in which the "service" of the pastor of souls is to be understood. The pastor is indeed sometimes presented as the servant of Christ: thus Peter, to whom the Lord entrusts his sheep:

> *Feed my sheep* (John 21:17). . . . When a pastor is about to entrust his own sheep to one of his servants, he will surely ask himself if the earnings of that servant are proportional to the value of his sheep. And so he would entrust his sheep to a qualified servant and would recoup from the servant's money the outlay he had made on the sheep that he bought with his own money. Well, then, here the Lord Christ, even as he entrusts to his servant the sheep that he has purchased with his own blood, assures himself of the qualifications of the servant by predicting for him suffering and the shedding of blood (Sermon 296, 4).

It is Christ, says Augustine in still another sermon, who feeds the souls of the faithful by means of the words of the preacher: "But we, who are we? His ministers, his servants.

What we bestow upon you is not our own; we draw it from his storeroom" (Sermon 229E, 4).

In Letter 228, 2, Augustine gives the simple reason for the grave responsibilities incumbent upon the bishops and clergy in the face of the calamities provoked by the barbarian invasions. The entire clergy must be ready even to sacrifice their lives, for they are "servants of Christ, ministers of his word and mystery."

But what does it mean to be servants of Christ, if not to serve those whom Christ came to save by making himself their servant? "You serve Christ well, if you serve those whom Christ has served" (*Expositions on the Psalms* 103, sermon 3, 9, 14).

Augustine admonishes a bishop on the day of his consecration: "What must first be understood by one who is set over the people is that he is the servant of many. Nor must he disdain this; he must not, I say, disdain to be the servant of many, for the Lord of lords did not disdain to serve us" (Sermon 340A, 1). And a little later in the same sermon: "Therefore, to put it briefly, we are your servants: your servants, but also your fellow servants. We are your servants, but all of us have one Lord. We are your servants, but in Jesus, as the Apostle says: *But we are your servants through Jesus*" (2 Corinthians 4:5) (Sermon 340A, 3).

Moreover, the bishop is in the service of the Church: "We are servants of his Church and most especially of the weakest members, whatever be our position as members of that same body" (*The Work of Monks* 29, 37).

From Saint Ambrose, Augustine had learned, among many other things, to minister with unremitting dedication to the "infirmities" of all who sought out the bishop; and he tells us it left him precious little time to nourish his body with food or his mind with reading (*Confessions* 6, 3, 3).

The Church is the house of God, of whose beauty Augustine is enamored and he pays tribute to that beauty, singing its praise with his voice (*Answer to the Writings of Petilian* 3, 1, 2). Possidius will praise his hero as "chief member of the body of the Lord . . . always solicitous and most vigilant for the good of the Church universal" (*Life* 18, 6).

Whenever and wherever one of the faithful turns to him for spiritual assistance, Augustine considers it his duty to place himself entirely at the service of the seeker. That marvelous little treatise on prayer, the Letter to Proba, begins with a dedication by Augustine of his intention of ministering, in the charity of Christ, to the pious desire of his correspondent (Letter 130, 1). And in another letter, he speaks of "that voluntary service he owes to the pious virgin Florentina" (Letter 266, 2). Not only to the members of the Church, but to non-Christians as well, "to all we owe, in some fashion, our free service" (*The Deeds of Pelagius* 16, 51).

But, seeing that Christ has entrusted to each individual bishop a particular portion of his flock, it is primarily to this particular Church that that bishop owes his service (Letter 134, 1). It is the Lord who has made him the servant of the people of Hippo (Letter 124, 2). Bishops and clergy are bound by the love of Christ to their ministry, so that they can never abandon the churches to which they owe their service (Letter 228, 1). It is their duty to adapt themselves to the customs and usages of the churches which they are serving (*The Work of Monks* 28, 37).

Augustine's whole time is devoted to this assignment of service to his Church, and the rare moments of relaxation he permits himself amid the press of duties are intended to restore his physical powers "needful to service we must render" (Letter 261, 1). Anyone who was close to Augustine, like Possidius, had constantly before him the lesson of that whole illustrious life, which Possidius sums up in these words reporting Augustine's own vision of his episcopal service: "I, too, the least among all the ministers of God, with that unfeigned faith (1 Timothy 1:5; 6:5) with which we ought to serve and please the Lord of Lords and all the good faithful . . ." (*Life* Preface, 3).

In the light of all this, it is scarcely necessary to note that Augustine did not think of service to the Church as signifying or connoting any campaign to maintain or increase the external power or prestige of an institution, though it would be difficult to find any more enlightened and passionate champion of the grandeur and splendor of the Church than Augustine himself. But the pastor of souls serves the Church when he serves, within the Church, the members of Christ, and the prodigality of his solicitude must be directly proportionate to the need or the weakness of his charges. This point will come out even more clearly when we study the spirit that Augustine felt must animate this service.

LET US HEAR HIS OWN VOICE

Augustine is not the man to base pastoral (or indeed any spiritual) attitudes on vague pious feelings or spineless conformism to popular opinion. He "who meditates day and night on the law of the Lord" (*Life* 3, 2) takes as the norm of his life the word of God. Thus his conception of the priesthood as a ministry in the sense of a service takes its inspiration from sacred Scripture, as is shown by his frequent reference to scriptural texts on this whole matter.

The chief scriptural source seems to be Matthew 20:26-28: *Whoever among you wants to be great must become the servant of you all, and if he wants to be first among you he must be your slave — just as the Son of Man has not come to be served but to serve, and to give his life to set many others free.* Sometimes Augustine refers to this text indirectly, without a literal citation, seeing in it the precept and example given by Jesus himself: "He does well, that is he behaves with humble charity and kindly severity, who commands the brethren, mindful the while of being himself their servant, as the Lord himself teaches by precept and example" (*Answer to the Letter of Parmenian* 3, 2 16).

Elsewhere Augustine cites the text with an extensive commentary, relating it to other passages of Scripture. This is the "harmony of Scriptures" technique, a favorite of the fathers. It delights in relating the most disparate texts, with no concern for historical or philological connections, seeing rather in their common divine inspiration the cogent argument in favor of their consonance and unity. Thus, in his commentary on Psalm 103:14: *You raise grass for the cattle, and vegetation for people's use,* Augustine notes that *the cattle* are human beings to whom the preachers are sent and that thus the two parts of the verse have the same meaning. Then he continues:

> Thus we are sent into service, not into freedom (servituti, non libertati). What, then, are we to make of the words: *It is to freedom that you have been called* (Galatians 5:13)? Well, just listen to what the same Apostle himself has to say: *For though I am no man's slave, yet I have made myself everyone's slave, that I might win more men and women to Christ* (1 Corinthians 9:19). And to the very ones whom he tells: *It is to freedom that you have been called* to those same ones he adds at once: "Be careful that freedom does not become mere opportunity for your lower nature. You should be free to serve each other in love." Those whom he had called free, he calls slaves; not in reference to their condition but in virtue of the redemption of Christ; not out of necessity but out of love. "In love," he says, "serve each other." And his meaning is that in the service we render one another we are serving Christ, not mere fragile people of flesh and blood. Was it not of him indeed that it was said that he served many well? The literal reference is to a prophet but the words are commonly understood of Christ (see Isaiah 53:11). But let us listen to his own voice in the gospel: *Whoever among you wants to be great,* he says, *must become the servant of all.* He whose blood has made you free has made you my servant. Hear that other voice that says: *We are your servants for the sake of Jesus* (2 Corinthians 4:5). Have an honest love for your servants, but in your Lord. May he grant us to serve you well. Because, whether we wish it or not, we are servants; yet if we ourselves do wish to be servants, then we are serving not out of necessity but out of love (*Expositions on the Psalms 103, sermon 3, 9*)

Although Augustine here expands his reflections to the state and status of every Christian in his relation with his fellow Christians, the point of departure shows his intentions of referring especially to the pastors called to exercise authority as a service of love.

Some of the passages we have already reported from the sermon delivered on the occasion of the consecration of a bishop. We must now return to a consideration of that sermon, with its express consideration of the pastoral office, omitting excerpts we have already cited:

When our Lord spoke to the apostles to confirm them in holy humility, after he had shown them a child as an example, he said to them: *Whoever wants to be greatest among you must be your servant.* There you see that I have not wronged my brother, your future bishop, in wishing and urging him to be your servant. For if I wronged him, I wronged myself first, for in speaking about a bishop, I speak not just as anyone but as a bishop; and what I urge him to do, I myself fear, remembering the words of the holy Apostle: *We are your servants through Jesus Christ.* Through him we are servants, through whom we are also free; it is he who tells those who believe in him: *If the Son sets you free, you will be truly free* (John 8:36). Shall I hesitate, then, to be a servant through him, since unless I became free through him I should remain lost in slavery? . . . Let us see, then, in what way the bishop who is put in command is a servant. In the same way as our Lord himself. For when he said to his apostles, *Whoever wants to be greatest among you must be your servant,* for fear that human pride might take offense at the name of servant, he quickly consoled them, and by giving himself as an example encouraged them to do what he had commanded. *Whoever wants to be greatest among you must be your servant.* But observe how: *As the Son of Man came not to be served but to serve. . . .* What does his saying mean then: *As the Son of Man came not to be served but to serve?* Listen to what follows: *He came not to be served but to serve, and to give his life as a ransom for many.* This is the meaning of our Lord's service; this is the kind of servant he commanded us to be. He gave his life as a ransom for many; he redeemed us. Which of us is fit to redeem anyone? It is his blood, his death that has redeemed us from death, his humility that has raised us from the ground, but we too have to make our own small contribution to his members because we have been made his members; he is the head and we are the body. So the apostle John urges us in his letter to follow the example of our Lord who had said, *Whoever wants to be greatest among you must be your servant; as the Son of Man came not to be served but*

> *to serve, and to give his life as a ransom for many;* therefore
> he urges us to do the same, saying: *Christ laid down his life
> for us, so we also ought to lay down our lives for each other*
> (1 John 3:16 — Sermon 340A, 2-3).

The various spiritual figures and phrases used by Augustine
to represent the mission of the bishop clearly show that his
basic conception of the priesthood as service is of scriptural
inspiration. It need hardly be said that these figures and
phrases are of much more than merely literary value in
Augustine's eyes. Under the veil of allegory is foreshadowed a
reality no less genuine than that which is expressed in formal
enunciation. It will suffice for our purpose simply to pass these
images and phrases in review, noting perhaps those instances
in which the element of service is more accentuated.

The bishop is like the innkeeper spoken of in the parable of
the Good Samaritan (Luke 10:35):

> The robbers have left you half dead on the road, but you
> have been found by the Good Samaritan who was passing
> by; you have had wine and oil poured upon you, you have
> received the sacrament of the Only-Begotten; you have
> been set upon his own mount, you have believed in Christ
> incarnate; you have been brought to the inn, you are in the
> care of the Church. That is why I am speaking. And what I
> do, we all do: our position is that of innkeeper (*stabularii
> fungimus munere*). To that innkeeper it was said: *I will pay
> you back whatever more you spend, when I come through
> here on my return.* If only we were at least spending our own
> earnings! But everything that we are expending, brethren, is
> the Lord's coin. We are your fellow servants; we, too, live
> from what serves to nourish the rest. Let no one attribute to
> us the good that he receives. We are wicked servants if we
> do not give it; and if we do give it, then we still cannot boast
> about that, seeing that we are not giving of our own. Let us
> all love him with all our heart; for him and through him and
> in him let us be united among ourselves! We all have but one
> King: may we all succeed in reaching the one kingdom!

With this vibrant peroration does Augustine conclude one of
his sermons (Sermon 179A, 7-8; see Sermon 46, 4, 76).

In another sermon, there is a brief Pauline text cited and
briefly commented on. It suggests another image of the

episcopal office, which Augustine barely develops: "Make our service (ministerium) fruitful. You are the field of God (1 Corinthians 3:19). Receive and welcome him who plants and waters from without, and within your hearts him who gives life to the seed" (Sermon 340, 1).

At somewhat greater length, in a letter addressed to the faithful of his diocese, Augustine uses the occasion of a question of charitable relief to give dramatic expression to his own feelings: "*It is not your gift that I long for but rather the fruit that will accrue to you from that gift* (Philippians 4:17). Rejoice my heart, therefore, for I long to enjoy your fruit. You are the plants of God, that he deigns to water abundantly by means of our ministry of service (ministerium)" (Letter 258, 3).

The bishop is likewise at the service of the people of God as overseer, which his very title implies him to be [*episkopos* in Greek; Augustine actually here uses the Latin form *superintentor* but it is merely a gloss on *episcopus*], "appointed by the Lord to take care of his vineyard" (*Expositions on the Psalms* 126, 3). This image is developed in Augustine's commentary on Ezekiel 33, where the reference is to the people selecting one of themselves and posting him as a sentry to stand guard for the country (Sermon 137, 15). This passage has been read in the assembly met to celebrate the anniversary of Augustine's consecration and he takes it as the topic of his sermon (Sermon 339). And Possidius gives us the reason impelling the bishop to the choice: "And this he did, considering himself to be a sentry posted by God for the house of Israel" (*Life* 19, 5).

This sermon interweaves the image of the scout (speculator) with that of manager (procurator) who is assigned to provide, out of his master's goods, the necessaries for the entire household. Augustine here takes his cue from the custom of offering a dinner to the poor in celebration of the anniversary of the bishop's consecration: "Today we have our fellow paupers to feed, and we must share our provisions with them, but as for you, these words of mine are your food. I have not enough to feed all with the bread which can be handled and seen. I feed you with what I feed on myself; I am a servant (minister), not the head of the family" (Sermon 339, 4).

Near the end of the sermon, Augustine again avails himself of this image to remind the faithful of the responsibility each one of them has before God alone: "Why do they wish me to promise what he does not? Supposing the agent offers you security. What use is that to you, if the head of the house forbids it? I am an agent, a servant" (Sermon 339, 9).

We have already reported a passage (Sermon 229E, 4) in which Augustine presents himself and his fellow bishops as "servants" precisely in the sense implied in the image of the manager or steward (see *Homilies on the Gospel of John* 46, 8, 27)

Finally, there is the sermon from which we have several times already cited excerpts, the sermon for the consecration of a bishop: "Now I speak to God's people in Christ's name, I speak in God's church, I speak as God's servant, whatever kind of person I am, but your hope must not be in us, your hope must not be in humanity. Whether good or bad, we are servants. But the good and faithful servants are truly servants" (Sermon 340A, 9).

THE MANNER OF THE SERVICE

The "service" of which Augustine so insistently speaks is, as we have seen, directed to the utility of the Church; consequently the variety of forms which that service will assume depends on the needs of the Church as such. This is Augustine's own criterion in all decision making. Thus he writes to Bishop Aurelius of Carthage: "After mulling over and over again in our mind what would be useful to the salvation of those whose servants we are in Christ to nurture them, I do not see any other solution" (Letter 60, 1).

The mandatory character of this service is specially stressed in the letter to Bishop Honoratus of Thiabe (Letter 228 already mentioned), in which Augustine indicates the cases and circumstances in which a bishop or other cleric may or must stay with the faithful or may flee before the barbarian invaders.

The words of Jesus: *When they persecute you in one town, take refuge in the next* (Matthew 10:23) certainly cannot be interpreted as though the Lord "had thereby intended that the flock bought with his blood should be left without the needed ministrations (ministerio), without which they cannot live" (Letter 228, 2). On the other hand, that hierarch is truly fulfilling the apostle John's admonition to give one's life for one's brothers (1 John 3:16) who "suffers precisely for not having been willing to abandon the brethren who need him for the health and salvation of their souls as Christians" (Letter 228, 3).

"He who is able to flee and does not flee, so as not to abandon the ministry and the service entrusted to him by Christ, without which ministry people can neither live as Christians nor become Christian —such a man is accomplishing a more generous work of charity than the man who flees, thinking not of his brothers and sisters but of himself, and who later, when captured, endures martyrdom rather than deny Christ" (Letter 228, 4). "Of course where there are no longer any who have need of their services, no one is saying that the servants should remain" (Letter 228, 5).

Paul in his flight from Damascus and Athanasius in his flight from Alexandria were both acting according to these norms (Letter 228, 6). But beyond all doubt "that minister is pitiless and wicked who snatches away the services of his ministry, needful to religion, precisely when those services are most needed" (Letter 228, 7). Therefore, "let no one so act that by his flight the ministerial services of the Church should be lacking, those services that are necessary and binding especially in such grave upheavals" (Letter 228, 12). Let the bishops and clerics tell the people just why they are staying: "If we stay here, we stay not on our own account but on yours, so as not to deprive you of any of the services that we know to be necessary for your salvation in Christ" (Letter 228, 13).

After his examination of the various cases, Augustine concludes in this vein: "Whoever flees under such circumstances that his flight entails no loss to the Church of needful services is governing himself by the command or at least by the permission of the Lord. But whoever flees under circumstances that leave the flock of Christ deprived of nourishment necessary to the spiritual life — such a one is that hireling who sees the wolf coming and flees because he has no interest in the sheep (John 10:10-13)" (Letter 228, 14). The concrete forms assumed by this service to the Church are well summed up in the passage already cited (Letter 228, 2): they are primarily the ministry of the word and of the mystery.

This dual form of the priestly ministry was already clear in Augustine's mind at the very outset of his own priestly life, when he defined the priest as "a man . . . who administers to the people the mystery and the word of God" (Letter 21, 3). Augustine recurs to this definition, when he has been ten years a bishop, to indicate the bishop's mission: "We are not bishops for ourselves but for those to whom we administer the word and the mystery of the Lord" (*Answer to Cresconius* 2, 9, 13). Thus, too, in his letter to Cornelius, Augustine justifies the severity he must apply to the old libertine by referring to himself as a "servant assigned to the service of the eternal city, of the divine word and mystery" (Letter 259, 2).

The "daily ministry of the body of the Lord" is necessary to the faithful especially in the hour of persecution, so that they may not fall victim to the wiles of the devil who is trying to seduce them into apostasy (Letter 218, 6). In such upheavals, too, there is an urgent and indispensable need of ministers for the administration of baptism and penance for consoling, edifying, exhorting (Letter 218, 8).

Augustine is much more insistent on the ministry of the word. We shall be returning later to a more detailed consideration of this essential activity of the pastor of souls; here we limit ourselves to noting a few passages which present it most clearly as a "service."

On 18 December 425, Augustine had been speaking to the faithful about his own preoccupations on the score of the behavior of some of the clergy sharing the common life with him; he mentions his own intentions in the matter of coping with the problems and concludes thus: "Pray for me that I may serve you in the work of God so long as my soul remains in this body, so long as I have any strength left at all" (Sermon 355, 7). In another sermon he begs his hearers to be attentive and to pray for him and he reminds them that he is serving the faithful with his preaching: "I want you to pay attention and pray for me that I may be able to say things useful to you. It may be that our thinking is our own affair, but whenever we speak, we are rendering service to you (vobis servimus)" (Sermon 8, 2).

He begins a sermon on the feast day of the martyrs, by saying that "we could not deny our service to this festive occasion today" even though he had already preached a lengthy sermon the day before (*Expositions on the Psalms* 63, 1, 6).

This theme is still more explicit in the beginning of a sermon on the feast day of Saint John the Baptist, a sermon delivered while Augustine was on the road:

> Today the Lord has willed to give you our voice and presence, my dear Christians, and in so doing he has consulted his own will and not our ideas in the matter. We render thanks to him in company with you and pay you the tribute of our word. This is our ministry in which it is right and fitting for us to serve you (in quo nos servire vobis et oportet et decet). It is now up to you, beloved, to garner lovingly what the servants of God can provide for you, and to give thanks together with us to him who has granted us the favor of spending this day in your midst (Sermon 293A, 1).

Indeed, "the preachers of the word are oxen and servants at once . . . oxen who thresh grain, men who serve" (*Expositions on the Psalms* 103, sermon 3, 10, 1).

The ministry of preaching is a service rendered to the gospel, for the salvation of others; it is directed to the redemption of the brethren and so everyone assigned to this ministry must stick to it, even overcoming, as did Saint Paul, the desire to be with Christ in eternal rest (see Philippians 1:21-26 — *Questions on the Gospels* 2, 13).

Augustine makes another brief reference to this ministry of service, when he prays: "Inspire, O my Lord and my God, inspire your servants, my brothers, your sons, my masters, whom I serve with my heart, my tongue, and my pen" (*Confessions* 9, 13, 37). The reference here to the pen points to still another form of service rendered by Augustine to the many who begged it of him, and to the countless multitudes of his own day and later ages, to all of whom his written words have brought and are still bringing a message of comfort and of hope.

These, then, are the forms of service most proper to the priestly office. But in addition, Augustine stresses, the priestly servant must be ready to accept other forms which are imposed by circumstances, even though they be not immediately directed to the salvation of souls.

Augustine's reference to the "customs and usages of the churches whose servants we are" (*The Work of Monks* 28, 37) is amply expanded by his biographer when he speaks of the burdensome judicial functions, the business of recommendations and of pleas to the civil authorities (*Life* 19-20). Augustine is outspoken in one sermon about just how burdensome these visits to the civil authorities were for him. Replying to stupid comments circulating in the community, Augustine paints a vivid picture of one of the most thankless aspects of the episcopal ministry:

> Often people say of us: "Why is he running to that official? What does the bishop want with that important person?" Now listen, you all know perfectly well that it is your own needs that compel us to go where we would rather not, to watch for the right moment, to stand in line at the door, to wait while the reputable and the disreputable alike are shown in, to get ourselves announced to be received at long last, and then to pour our heart out in pleading, bearing in silence the humiliations heaped upon us, and for all our pains to succeed only sometimes, while others time we have to go away disgruntled (Sermon 301, 17).

But whatever may be the specific modalities of the daily ministry, there must always be "heart" in it, as the passage from the *Confessions* cited above insists. For more important than all the details of external activity is the spirit that animates the whole work. "Let us love the inner things more than the outer; let us find our joy in those inner things; as for the outer things, let us devote ourselves to them as necessity dictates, not from free choice" (*Expositions on the Psalms* 139, 15, 45).

THE MOTIVES ANIMATING THE SERVICE

The Augustinian texts already cited have shown us clearly enough that his vision of the priestly commission as "a service" rendered to the Church "in the gospel," "in Christ," is deeply rooted in and sustained by an enlightened faith that pervades every aspect of the activity of the man who is unreservedly consecrated to God. Some other texts will help us to a better understanding of the spirit in which Augustine believes the minister of God to be called to perform his daily duty. This spirit should be a compound of obedience, unselfishness, humility, and Christian love.

Obedience

The servant and minister of God must work in obedience to the will of God who has imposed the service. In a letter excusing himself for not having gone to pay a visit to Albinus, Pinanus, and Melania, the illustrious Roman patricians who had come to Africa, Augustine assures them that it was not the cold, unusually bitter though it had been that winter, that had held him back, but solely his duty as pastor. "The people of Hippo, to whom the Lord has given me as servant" are in such straits that it is not permissible for the bishop to go away even for a brief visit, says Augustine (Letter 124, 2).

The same thing is said even more openly at the beginning of Book 10 of the Confessions (10, 3, 6), where Augustine indicates one of his aims in writing this work: "These are your servants and my brothers, whom you have willed to be your sons and my masters, whom you have ordered me to serve, if I wish to live with you from you. . . . To this I attend in deed and word. . . . To those, therefore, whom you order me to serve, I shall make known not what manner of man I used to be but rather what manner of man I am henceforth and shall be forevermore."

To the accusation of ambitious designs, Augustine replies with a vigorous protest: "God is my witness: all this activity forced upon me by the government of the Church, wherein some think it is my ambition to dominate, I put up with it because of the service I owe to the love of the brethren and the fear of God, but I am not enamored of it" (Letter 126, 9).

The same rule he follows in his dealings with the whole body of the faithful, primarily his own diocese, he follows likewise in his dealings with the individuals who come to him for help. Thus, Augustine says that he has been moved to heed the request of the tribune Marcellinus, on the one hand out of Christian love, on the other out of a fear of offending God "who had inspired in you such a desire: in rendering you this service I shall be serving him who has inspired that desire in you" (*The Merits and Forgiveness of Sins* 1, 1, 1).

The persuasion that in serving the brethren he is fulfilling the will of God makes Augustine realize just how serious and heavy is the responsibility attached to this service. He feels it to weigh upon him like a full pack on the back of a soldier (sarcina); he deems it a dangerous business (periculosa ratio) of which he must render an account to God.[4]

Unselfishness

No slightest remnant of selfish concern or ambition can be allowed to remain in the man who is called by God to serve the Church: He must be a paragon of unselfishness in the fulfillment of his service and the discharge of his duties, working, as Saint Paul admonishes, *not for his own interests but for those of Jesus Christ* (Philippians 2:21). Possidius sees this unselfishness perfectly embodied in Augustine (*Life* 19, 1).

"Those men are wicked and iniquitous servants who have enriched themselves at the expense of the Lord's flock,

---

4. See Michele Pellegrino, "S. Agostino, pastore d'anime," in *Recherches Augustiniennes,* volume I, Paris, 1958, pages 321-323.

dividing up what they had not bought. They have truly been the unfaithful servants who have divided up the flock of Christ and have fattened their own purses, so to speak, by fleecing his flock; and you heard them say: *Those are my sheep.*" But, says Augustine, let them hear and heed the warning of Christ: "Those that I have bought, where are they? Wicked servants, to call the sheep yours, to lay claim to what I have bought, when they would have perished, had I not bought them" (Sermon 313A, 2). These are the wicked shepherds, the hirelings against which Augustine rails so often in his commentaries on the denunciations of the prophets and of Christ himself (see Sermon 46).

The ultimate root of the obligation of absolute unselfishness on the part of the pastor of souls is, for Augustine, the fundamental theological tenet of the absolute necessity and gratuity of grace. Since being a pastor is likewise a grace, the pastor must seek no other recompense for his labors, saving him only who is the pastor's first and peerless love (Sermon 340, 1).

This total neglect of his own interests must impel him if the need arises, to the sacrifice even of his very life, Augustine reminds us, citing the words and example of Jesus who came not to be served but to serve and to give his life to set many free (Matthew 20:28), and Augustine reinforces this text with a reference to Saint John's admonition to imitate Christ (1 John 3:16).

Trained as he was by long pastoral experience to see in their concrete reality the conditions and needs prevailing in the Church, and free of any preoccupation not directed solely to the fulfillment of the humble and generous service to souls, Augustine does not hesitate to praise certain bishops who renounce their office for higher motives. He touches on this point in his argument with Cresconius on the way the Catholic Church treats bishops or other clerics ordained in the Donatist schism when they return to her communion. The deciding factor must always be what most redounds to the peace and profit of the Church: "Indeed we are not bishops for ourselves but for those to whom we administer the word and the mystery of the Lord; and so we ought to be or not be bishops, according as the needs of those whom we govern shall dictate, provided there be no danger of scandal, seeing that we are bishops not for ourselves but for the others." And at this point he mentions the bishops who have stepped down: "Certain men, endowed with holy humility, have laid down the episcopal office, motivated by a sincere sense of faith and piety, because of some shortcomings of theirs that caught the eye of others; and in this not only did they commit no fault, they even merited praise." And Augustine goes on to counter possible objections in advance by saying that, just as a man may have good reasons for not accepting the episcopate in the first place, so he may also have good reasons for renouncing it later (*Answer to Cresconius* 2, 11, 13).

A similar line of thought is to be found in a letter written five or six years later to the tribune Marcellinus preparatory to the great Synod of Carthage in June of 411. Concerned to safeguard the honor and dignity of the Donatist bishops, should the meeting issue in the hoped-for restoration of Church unity, Augustine proposes that in every diocese the bishop who has returned from Donatism shall keep his position side by side with his Catholic fellow bishop; and in the event that the people are not willing to accept the two bishops, both shall retire in order to set the stage for the election of a single pastor.

> How can we hesitate to offer to our Redeemer the sacrifice of this act of humility? He came down from heaven into a human body so that we might be members of him. And shall we be afraid to come down from the bishop's chair to prevent his members from being torn by a cruel division? As for us, let us be faithful and obedient Christians and that is enough for us and more than enough: let us be so always. But the fact that we are consecrated bishops, that regards the Christian people; let us, then, do with our episcopate what will help the Christian people in the direction of Christian peace. If we are profitable servants, why would we prejudice the eternal interest of the Lord with an eye to our own temporal prestige (Letter 128, 3).

This document was read to the plenary assembly of almost 300 Catholic bishops prior to the conference. It was a somewhat unexpected joy to Augustine and the other supporters of the idea to discover that all enthusiastically agreed to the proposal, except two: one old bishop who soon changed his mind under the fraternal reproof of all his fellows; and one other bishop who nevertheless finally came round to giving his assent as well (*Proceedings with Emeritus* 6).

Since it is our aim in these pages to lay special stress on those points on which Augustine can even today serve as our master and our model, we may here be permitted to draw attention to the applicability of the passages just quoted to our own day and situation. The up-to-date experts may find such considerations as Augustine has here set forth to be abstract and far removed from the complex reality of our own day; yet we believe that these considerations can give useful pointers on how best to solve major problems, by following Augustine in taking as supreme norm and criterion for the life of the Church not outmoded customs or private interests but those ultimate principles wherein the Church sees the deepest reason for its existence and its activity.

On the other hand, Augustine is just as firm in asserting the duty incumbent upon the pastor of souls to remain at his post, even if that involves sacrificing his own peace of mind. When Peter, after the miraculous catch of fish, cried to Jesus: *Depart from me, Lord, for I am a sinful man* (Luke 5:8), the Lord paid no heed to him; which "means that good and spiritually minded men ought not to cultivate such tendencies so as to let themselves become perturbed by the sins of the people and to abandon their ecclesiastical office in the quest for a safe and quiet life" (*Questions on the Gospel* 2, 2).

Humility

It is therefore an act of humility that Augustine requests, in the name of Christ, from Christ's ministers. For if there is one bent of soul proper to the man called to serve, it is precisely this sincere humility, amounting to an adoration of God whose will is being done, in the relations of that servant with the brethren to whom he is offering his own service.

This theme quite naturally comes out in many of the passages already cited. Let us here recall a favorite theme of Augustine, who was fond of distinguishing between two different marks of a bishop: the mark of a Christian, which he shares with all the faithful; and the mark of a bishop which makes him their head and chief. The first is a motive of consolation, the second is a motive of alarm.

> For you I am a bishop; with you I am a Christian. The first is the name of the office I have undertaken, the second of grace; the first of danger, the second of salvation. . . . So if the fact that I have been redeemed with you delights me more than the fact that I have been set over you, then, as our Lord commands, I shall be more tirelessly your servant, for fear of being ungrateful for the redemption which made me worthy to be your fellow servant (Sermon 340, 1).

This is a constantly recurring term in Augustine to indicate the bond of community between bishop and faithful: fellow servant, *conservus*. To the monks, to whom this title is specially appropriate in view of their common vow (*propositum*) of an ascetic life, Augustine writes: "If we are brothers, if you are our sons, if we are fellow servants, or rather your servants in Christ, listen to our admonitions, accept our precepts, take what we offer you" (*The Work of Monks* 29, 37). The term must have been quite current in Hippo in those days, for Possidius uses it quite spontaneously: "I recall even today, and not I myself only but also the other of my brothers and fellow servants, that there were then living with us and with that holy man in the Church of Hippo . . ." (*Life* 15, 1).

The commonly shared vocation and, in the sense already indicated, the common bond with Christ is expressed in other terms as well, equally evangelical in flavor. Even the bishop is but one of the Lord's sheep, fellow disciple together with the rest of the faithful: "In virtue of the office entrusted to us, we are your guardians, but we ourselves desire to be guarded together with you. For you we are as shepherds, but under that Good Shepherd we are sheep together with you. In this, our office, we are for you as masters; but under that One Master, in this school we are your fellow disciples" (*Expositions on the Psalms* 126, 3, 44).

In that sermon for the consecration of a bishop, which we have cited several times already, it is precisely from this title of fellow disciple that Augustine draws a lesson of humility for bishop and faithful alike:

> Who is the bishop who is called and is not one? He who rejoices in that honor rather than the salvation of God's flock, who in that high office seeks his own ends, not those of Jesus Christ. He is called a bishop, but is not a bishop, the name is no use to him. But no one calls him anything else. Have you seen the bishop? Have you greeted the bishop? They say, Where have you come from? The bishop. Where are you going? To the bishop. Therefore to be worthy of his name, let him listen not to me but with me. Let us listen together, and as fellow pupils in one school let us learn together from the one master, Christ, whose chair is in heaven because his cross was first on earth. He has taught us the way of humility: descending to ascend, visiting those who lay in the lowest depths, and raising those who wanted to be united to him (Sermon 340A, 4).

Love

The humility Jesus teaches us is therefore directed to the salvation of those for whom he humbled himself. That humility is inspired by love. And so anyone in command of the brethren and yet mindful that he is himself their servant will behave with humble charity (*humili caritate*) in the happy phrase of Augustine already cited (*Answer to the Letter of Parmenian* 3, 2 16). May the writer be permitted to recall here, in grateful admiration, a bishop who was a marvelous embodiment of the pastoral ideal proposed by Augustine. Angelo Soracco, bishop of Fossano from 1935 to 1943, made those words *humili caritate* the motto of his episcopal coat of arms, even as they were the faithful expression of his own attitude of mind and heart in the all too brief period of his pastoral ministry, cut short by his untimely death at barely 53 years of age.

In commenting on the Pauline admonition: *Keep out of debt altogether, except that perpetual debt of love which we owe one another* (Romans 13:8), Augustine shows how service is a consequence of love: "Indeed it is the love itself that demands the duty: if we are obeying the dictates of brotherly love, we shall be aiding to the limit of our powers anyone who justly desires our aid" (Letter 110, 5). The fear of Christ and the love of Christ oblige the bishop to serve the members of Christ. Even when he goes away on a journey, he does so not at his own whim but in order to render a needed service (Letter 122, 1).

It may seem that it is beyond the powers of a mere man to face up to the grave perils involved in not abandoning his post of duty: "It is possible where the supernatural love of God is brightly burning and the worldly passions are not smoldering. This love says: *Do you think anyone is weak without my feeling his weakness? Does anyone have his faith upset without my longing to restore him?* (2 Corinthians 11:29)" (Letter 228, 7). Augustine expresses the hope that there will spring up a generous competition among the ministers and servants of God to outdo one another in assisting, even at the risk of their own lives, the faithful threatened by the invaders; and this will happen, says Augustine, when both those who must remain and those who must flee "are burning with love and when both groups are pleasing to him who is love" (Letter 228, 12).

When it is offered willingly, our service is the fruit not of necessity but of Christian love (*Expositions on the Psalms* 103, sermon 3, 9, 63). And so Augustine can speak of a free service (*libera servitus*) which he owes to the faithful. This service is free inasmuch as it is freely accepted and performed out of love.

We have given such detailed treatment to this notion of "service" because it seems to us absolutely central to Augustine's vision of the priesthood and most productive for anyone interested in inspecting the various modalities of priestly activity and the interior attitudes that ought to direct and animate it. We do not here intend to ascribe to Augustine an originality of thought he would not himself admit, since, as we have seen, he draws this whole conception from his meditation on the word of God and the example of the Prince of pastors. Rather it seems pertinent here to point out the fact that this vision of the priestly ministry has been and is still present and operative in the Church, in the marvelous dedication, compounded of humility, sacrifice, and love, with which countless pastors have served and are serving souls.

We are happy to cite, in conclusion of this chapter, as a witness to the perennial vitality and fruitfulness of this idea, the words of Pope John XXIII, in his last Christmas radio broadcast in 1962, summing up the motivation of everything he had done during his pontificate, especially for the unremitting furthering of world peace at every opportunity: "The effort that has been our constant companion in these four years of our humble service, as we have seen that service and shall see it to the last moment, is the effort to be the servant of the servants of the Lord, who is truly the Lord and Prince of peace."

5

The Service of
Our Heart and Our Tongue

As "SERVANT OF THE CHURCH" the bishop or the priest must
devote all his powers to the Church's good, in the exercise of a
plethora of duties that cannot be defined in detail in advance,
but are suggested to him in each case by the different needs
confronting the people of God and by that Christian love that
impels the shepherd of souls to try to cope with all the needs of
his flock.

Yet Augustine for all his incessant round of most varied
activities always keeps in mind a clear-cut hierarchy of values
that gives a definite shape to his ministry. The two essential
dimensions of that ministry are the "mystery" and the "word"
of God. F. van der Meer's excellent study, *Saint Augustine,
Pastor of Souls,* has an admirable and thorough treatment of
Augustine's liturgical activities and his most zealous work at
dispensing God's grace in the administration of the sacraments.
We shall now proceed to a more detailed examination of the
second dimension of the priestly life as Augustine saw it and,
above all, lived it, namely the ministry of God's word.
Concerning this dimension of Augustine's priesthood we have
a mass of information at our disposal: his own frequent
references to it in his various writings, and above all the rich
harvest of sermons garnered for us by the devotion of his
hearers.

THE POWER OF THE WORD OF GOD IS GREAT

"My powers are but limited, O my brethren, but the power of the word of God is great. May that power work mightily in your hearts!" These words of one of his sermons (42, 1) show us quite clearly why Augustine set such great store by the ministry of preaching; he trusted implicitly in the power of the word of God.

This phrase "word of God" is for Augustine no mere conventional, timeworn synonym for preaching. He is acutely conscious of being the bearer of a word that is not his own, "What we are about to say," he begins another sermon, "comes, as we well know, not from us but from God" (Sermon 51, 1). And he begins still another sermon in the same tone: "The holy gospel we have just heard read has directed our attention to the remission of sins. About this subject we must now speak to you. We are indeed ministers of the word: not our own, of course, but that of God and of our Lord" (Sermon 114, 1). And so Augustine does not hesitate to call the preacher "tongue of God" (*Expositions on the Psalms* 27, 1).

On other occasions (obviously involving no modification of doctrinal meaning), Augustine calls preaching the "word of Christ" (even as the scripture of which preaching is the explanation). In commenting on Psalm 50:3, he says:

> *God will come openly, our God and he will not be silent!* He was not silent when he spoke through the mouth of the patriarchs; he was not silent when he spoke through his own mouth of flesh. And today, were he to be silent, would he not speak through the mouth of scripture? The reader has gone up to his place; it is God who is not silent. The preacher speaks: if he speaks in accord with truth, it is Christ who is speaking. Were Christ to be silent, I would not be here to tell you these things. But on your lips, too, he is not silent; when you were chanting, it was he who was speaking. He is not silent, but we must listen to him with the ear of the heart, for it is an easy thing to listen with the ear of flesh (Sermon 27, 1).

The person of the preacher is of little account. Whoever he may be, Christ himself speaks through his mouth. Augustine reminds his congregation of this truth in order to exhort them to listen attentively, even when the sermon is being given by a priest rather than the bishop himself: "We exhort you, dear Christians, to be good enough to listen diligently and attentively to the words of God which are going to be dispensed to you by the priests. The Lord our God is indeed truth itself, and you are listening to him, no matter who is serving as his mouthpiece" (Sermon 20, 5).

The preachers communicate the word of Christ to the faithful and so they are the voice of the Lord. In this sense does Augustine explain Psalm 19:5: *Their voice is gone out through all the earth, and their message to the ends of the earth.* This is said of the apostles, points out Augustine, the *heavens* that *declare the glory of God.* At Pentecost the apostles were filled with the Holy Spirit and made their voices resound not only in the place where they themselves were, but throughout the whole earth. "In this same Spirit and through him, we, too, speak here; for that voice has reached us, too, that voice that is gone out through all the earth, even if the heretic is not willing to come into the Church." The Church, continues the preacher, is the tent which the Lord has pitched in the sun, that is, rendered manifest to the Lord (*Expositions on the Psalms* 18, sermon 2, 5-6).

NATURE OF THE WORD OF GOD AND PREACHER

The nature, value, and efficacy of the word of God — all these are constantly recurring themes in Augustine, who illustrates them by using various figures, calculated to present the truth in concrete language, adapted to the capacities of his hearers. None of these images is an original invention of Augustine; all are taken from scripture, interpreted allegorically, in that "spiritual" meaning so dear to the Alexandrine school of patristic exegetes.

Food

The word of God is *food;* it is the *bread* of souls. The first of these figures is extensively developed in the sermon we have already quoted, which Augustine preached on the anniversary of his own consecration and in which he builds his exposition on the custom of offering a dinner to the poor on such occasions:

> Today we have our fellow paupers to feed, and we must share our provisions with them, but as for you, these words of mine are your food. I have not enough to feed all with the bread which can be handled and seen: I feed you with what I feed on myself; I am a servant, not the head of the family; what I set before you comes from the same source as I live from myself, from our Lord's storeroom, from the feasts given by that head of the family who *for us became poor, though he was rich, that we ourselves might become rich by his poverty* (2 Corinthians 8:9). If I set bread before you, after the bread was broken you would each take away a tiny piece of it; and even if I put out a great quantity, each of you would get very little. But as for what I say now, all of you possess the whole of it, and each of you possesses the whole of it (Sermon 339, 4).

Bread

The word of God is the *bread* with which the owner feeds his workers. He entrusts it to the heads of the Church who in their turn hand it out to the faithful:

> Let us now labor in the vineyard, let us await the end of the day. He who has engaged us to work will not abandon us, so that we shall not want. He feeds the worker who labors, even as he prepares to give that worker the reward at the end of the day. Even so does the Lord feed us while we are toiling in this world, not only with food for the belly but with food for the mind as well. If he were not there to feed you, I would not be here to speak to you. If I do this, delivering him not to your bellies but to your minds, it is because he feeds you with the word. You are hungry and you receive; you feast royally and you applaud.[1] What point would there be

---

1. It was not uncommon for the congregation to break out into enthusiastic applause of the preacher.

> to your acclamations, had no food reached your mind? But
> we — what are we? His ministers, his servants. What we
> bestow on you is not our own; we draw it from his
> storeroom. We ourselves live on it, for we are fellow
> servants (Sermon 229E, 4).

"What I am handing out to you is not my own. I eat of what
you eat; I live on what you live on. We have a common
storeroom in heaven; it is from there that the word of God
comes" (Sermon 95, 1).

Being a supernatural food, the word of God does not
become less because many eat of it; it is the "word" of God
himself on whom the angels feed and who has come down into
the womb of the Virgin.

> You stand attentive to listen to my words. As I speak, I am
> nourishing and feeding your souls. Were I to have brought
> you a material food, you would have divided it up among
> you and it could not have come through whole to each of
> you; rather, the more of you there were, into so many the
> more pieces would it have had to be divided, and the share
> of each would have been less, the greater the multitude that
> received it. Now I say to you: receive, take, eat. You have
> received, you have eaten, and you have not done any
> dividing up. Whatever I say is there whole for all and whole
> for each. So the power of the word of a mere man is beyond
> explanation; would any of you be able to tell me what is the
> word of God? The word of God nourishes thousands upon
> thousands of angels. In their mind they are fed, in their mind
> they are filled. That word fills the angels, fills the world, fills
> the womb of the Virgin: That Word is not dilated nor is that
> Word constricted. What is the Word of God? He himself
> has said it. Terse is his utterance but mighty his meaning: *I
> and the Father are one* (John 10:30 – Sermon 237, 4).

Elsewhere, too, Augustine identifies the bread of the word
of God with Christ, the Living Bread come down from heaven,
manifested to us in the gospel, to be searched out by us in the
prophets (*Expositions on the Psalms* 138, 1).

The better the preacher has prepared himself by a holy life
and by meditation on the scripture, the more solid and more
delicious will be the bread he can proffer to the faithful. Milan
was fortunate in this respect in having "the Bishop Ambrose,

famed the world over as one of the best, and your devoted
servant. In those days his eloquence tirelessly distributed to
your people the choicest of wheat, the joy of your oil, and the
sober intoxication of your wine" (*Confessions* 5, 13). Augustine's figure of the word of God as food leads him likewise to
speak very often of the assembly of the faithful as seated at a
banquet.[2]

Light

The word of God is *light*. Augustine develops this figure
from Psalm 76:5:

> *You who shine forth marvelously from the everlasting
> mountains.* Who are the everlasting mountains? Those
> whom he himself makes everlasting, the high mountains,
> the preachers of the truth. It is you who shine forth, but from
> the everlasting mountains. The high mountains are the first
> to receive your light; and your light as caught by the
> mountain engulfs the earth in its radiance. The high
> mountains are the apostles who have received, so to speak,
> the first fruits of the light in its rising (*Expositions on the
> Psalms* 75, 7).

Water

The word of God is pure and clear *water* to be given by the
shepherd-pastor to the thirsty sheep (Sermon 128, 7). In this
world, man is, as it were,

> in a desert land, trackless and waterless. . . . If only there
> were at least some water to refresh the stranded traveler. O
> fearful, dreadful, baleful desert! Yet God has indeed had
> pity on us and has opened us up a highway through the
> desert, our Lord Jesus Christ himself (John 14:6). He had
> prepared a consolation for us in the desert, by sending us the

---

2. Homilies on the First Letter of John 1, 12; Sermon 28, 2; Sermon
125, 8; Sermon 126, 8; Sermon 145, 2; Sermon 316, 1; Sermon 104,
5; Expositions on the Psalms 32, sermon 2, 1; Expositions on the
Psalms 103, sermon 1, 1; Sermon 1, 19; Expositions on the Psalms
120, 15; Expositions on the Psalms 141, 1.

preacher of his word; he has given us water in the desert, by
filling his preachers with his own Spirit, so that in them we
should have a *fountain of water welling up into eternal life*
(John 4:14 – *Expositions on the Psalms* 62:8).

The preachers are the fountains of water spoken of in Psalm
17:16 (*Expositions on the Psalms* 17, 16).

Rain

The word of God is a *rain* that comes down on the ground to
produce good fruits if that ground be good, thorns if it be bad.
With this thought, Augustine ends one sermon: "We have
spoken according to the gift that the Lord has given us. And all
that we say to you in the name of God — for it is God who
speaks through us — is a rain of God (*imber Dei*). It is up to
you to see to it what kind of ground you are. For when the rain
comes down on the ground it produces good fruits if the ground
is good, thorns if the ground is bad. Yet the rain falls as
beneficently over the thorns as over the fruits" (*Expositions
on the Psalms* 98, 15). In the rain that the heavenly Father
sends down "upon the just and the unjust alike," Augustine is
fond of seeing a "watering with the doctrine of truth" (*The
Lord's Sermon on the Mount* 1, 77).

Cloud

It is quite a natural transition from the figure of the rain to
that of the *cloud* from which the rain falls. Indeed, for all
practical purposes, the two figures are identical. The fathers
are all quite familiar with the scriptural symbolism of "clouds"
as a figure of the prophets, the apostles, and the preachers; and
it is well known to Augustine: "Not only the prophets but all
those who water souls with the word of God can be called
clouds. When they are ill understood, God *rain downs coals
of fire and brimstone on the wicked*; but when they are
understood well, he fertilizes the pious and faithful hearts"
(*Expositions on the Psalms* 10, 10).

Commenting on Psalm 36:6, Augustine says:

> *In the heavens is your mercy and your truth reaches to the clouds.* Who could know the heavenly mercy of God, did not God himself proclaim it to all? How has he proclaimed it? By sending his truth to the clouds. What clouds? The preachers of the word of God. . . . As far as the clouds has come the truth of God. And so there could be proclaimed to us the mercy of God which is in heaven and not on earth. And in every truth, my brethren, the preachers of the truth are clouds. When God threatens through the mouth of the preachers, his thunder rumbles athwart the clouds. When God works miracles through the instrumentality of the preachers, his lightning flashes athwart the clouds; he uses the clouds to strike terror into hearts and the rain to water them. Thus are these preachers, by whose mouth is preached the gospel of God, in very truth God's clouds. Let us therefore wait trustingly upon the mercy, the mercy that is in heaven I mean (*Expositions on the Psalms* 35, 8, 6).

"That phrase of the Lord, *When you see a cloud in the west,* signifies his flesh rising from death: for from that holy flesh is indeed poured down upon the whole earth the rain of the preaching of the gospel" (*Questions on the Gospel* 2, 27).

Augustine sees the same meaning in the verse *Your mercy is exalted to the heavens and your truth to the clouds.* He says:

> By clouds we understand the preachers of the truth, men who are bearers of what we might call this cloudy flesh, from which God lightnings with miracles and thunders with precepts. They are those clouds of which Isaiah speaks in the name of the Lord, in his denunciation of the unprofitable and barren vineyard that yielded only thorns: *I shall command my clouds that they rain not upon it,* that is, command my apostles to abandon the Jews and not to proclaim the gospel to them, but rather to proclaim it in the good earth of the Gentiles, from which spring up not thorns but grapes. We know then that the clouds of God are the preachers of the truth, the prophets, the apostles, all those who proclaim aright the word of truth and have within them a hidden light, even as the clouds have, from which flash the lightnings. The clouds, then, are men (*Expositions on the Psalms* 56, 17, 20).

Even as the cloud appears of little account and yet has hidden within it a mysterious power that flashes forth in the lightning, so the apostles (and the other preachers of the truth) appear weak and insignificant as men but are the bearers of a splendor that reveals itself in word and in miracles (*Expositions on the Psalms* 96, 8).

In the manna, that "bread of angels" eaten by man when God *commanded the clouds above and opened the door of heaven* (Psalm 78:23-25), Augustine discerns him

> who is in very truth the bread of angels, nourished as they are incorruptibly by the incorrruptible word of God. That man might be able to eat that bread, he *became flesh and dwelt among us* (John 1:14). It is this bread, indeed, that rains upon the whole world from the clouds of the gospel. And the hearts of the preachers open, like the door of heaven, as it were, and the word is preached, not to the synagogue that murmurs and tempts him, but to the Church that believes and fixes her hope in him (*Expositions on the Psalms* 77, 17, 3).

In his commentary on Psalm 104:3 (*Who has established a cloud for his going up*) Augustine feels his way through a somewhat more tortuous development of this same figure. First he admits that the verse in question can be quite literally understood of the ascension of Christ, but then he remarks that the clouds are the preachers, by whose instrumentality the faithful can ascend to the heaven of the scriptures:

> May the Lord my God deign to make even me one of those clouds, any one! He can see what a cloudy cloud I am. Still, you are supposed to see all preachers of the truth as clouds. All those whose weakness prevents them from ascending on their own to this heaven which is the understanding of the scriptures, ascend by means of the clouds. It may be happening to you this very day. If I am in fact getting anywhere, if my sweat and toil are not proving unprofitable, you are this minute ascending to the heaven of the divine scriptures, I mean to the understanding of them, by means of this my preaching. . . . Those very words that we have cited: *Who has established a cloud for his going up* — those very words you have understood with the aid of my preaching; now the clouds do not rain of their own power (*Expositions on the Psalms* 103, sermon 1, 11).

This theme is more extensively developed in Augustine's commentary on Psalm 89:7: *Who among the clouds can compare with the Lord?* Augustine first remarks that this text would not mean much were it taken literally. Then he asserts: "We understand, brethren, that these clouds, like the heavens [a reference to his commentary on the preceding verse: *The heavens declare your marvels*], are the preachers of the truth: the prophets, the apostles, the proclaimers of the word of God." And he backs up his interpretation by citing Isaiah 5:6-7 (which we have encountered above). Augustine goes on to say that the apostles turned to the Gentiles after raining unprofitably upon the Jews; and he sets out to show the meaning of the figures:

> They are at once "heavens" and "clouds": "heavens" in virtue of the splendor of the truth, "clouds" in virtue of that truth's being hidden in the flesh. All clouds are indeed tenuous because of the mortality with which they form and pass. . . . You see at this moment what a man is saying but you do not see what he carries in his heart; you see what the cloud presents to view, not what it keeps stored within. What eyes indeed can penetrate a cloud? Thus the clouds are the preachers of the truth who live in the flesh. . . . We are called clouds because of the flesh and we are preachers of the truth in virtue of the rain that comes down from the clouds.

Christ, the Word Incarnate, is himself likewise a cloud, but in a vastly different sense from his merely human preachers.[3]

Since lightning bolts flash forth from clouds, the preacher of the word of God is likened to these as well.

> *The clouds have uttered a voice* (Psalm 77:18). What clouds? Those God mentions when he is threatening the vineyard that has produced thorns instead of grapes and

---

3.   Expositions on the Psalms 88, sermon 1, 7-10; Expositions on the Psalms 45, 10, 16; Expositions on the Psalms 59; Expositions on the Psalms 59, 12, 11; Expositions on the Psalms 64, 14, 3; Expositions on the Psalms 66, 8; Expositions on the Psalms 67, 2, 17; Expositions on the Psalms 71, 19, 29; Expositions on the Psalms 95, 11, 4; 95, 14, 4; Expositions on the Psalms 146, 15; Sermon 181, 2; On Genesis: A Refutation of the Manichaeans 2, 5-6; Notes on Job 37.

when he says: *I shall command my clouds that they rain not upon the earth* (Isaiah 5:6). There are the apostles leaving Judaea to go out to the Gentiles. Among all the nations, *the clouds uttered a voice;* preaching Christ, *the clouds uttered a voice, your lightning bolts shot forth.* Those he had called voices of the clouds, he now calls lightning bolts. These are but likenesses. Properly speaking, indeed, the lightning bolt is not the rain, nor the rain the lightning bolt. But the word of God is a lightning bolt in that it strikes, and it is rain, in what it waters (*Expositions on the Psalms* 76, 19-29).

Winds

The *winds* in Psalm 135:7 (*Who raises up clouds from the ends of the earth, brings the winds out of his storehouse*) signify for Augustine the preachers in the spiritual reality of their mission: "The preachers are at once, I think, both clouds and winds: clouds, by reason of the flesh; winds, by reason of the spirit (a pun by Augustine on the ambivalent 'spiritus'). Clouds indeed are seen, winds are heard but not seen" (*Expositions on the Psalms* 87, 10, 66).

Physician

The preacher is a *physician.* "The excellent preachers of the word of God . . . act upon people as do the great physicians, who themselves cannot raise the dead, unless the grace of God brings them back to life again" (*Expositions on the Psalms* 87, 10, 66).

Seed

The word of God is a *seed* which the preacher casts into the hearts of the faithful as into ground variously disposed. Just as a field must be sown before it can bear fruit, so too "the most necessary rule for Christian behavior is to listen to the word of God," so as to gain salvation from him who one day must sit in judgment. To this end, "you must keep up your scriptural readings every day, so that the evils of this world may take no root in your heart nor the thorns smother the seed that has been sown in you. So, too, the word of God must be repeated to you over and over again, so that you do not forget it and go around saying that you have never heard what we insist we have said" (Sermon 5, 1).

This same theme is developed in Augustine's commentary on Acts 17:18. He misunderstands *spermologos,* the nickname given Saint Paul by the Athenians, and takes it to mean "word sower." "So did they dub him in scorn but believers do not reject that title. Indeed he was, in very truth, a sower of words and a reaper of good conduct. Even we ourselves, tiny as we are and unworthy of being compared to his greatness, even we go about sowing the words of God and hoping for an abundant harvest from your behavior" (Sermon 150, 1; Sermon 101, 1).

Augustine finds the transition quite natural from this to the "sower of the gospel, of whom the Lord speaks (Matthew 13:1), for such indeed was Paul." "Had he hesitated to cast the seeds, fearing that some might fall by the wayside, some among thorns, some upon stones, the seed would never have been able to reach the good ground. Let us also be openhanded in our sowing, and do you prepare your hearts and bear fruit" (Sermon 101, 3). Hence the preacher's distrust of the proud philosopher, who resembles the mockers of Paul: "I sow as my poor powers permit, since I am a sower of words. I sow. What I sow falls into you as upon hard ground. I am not slothful and I find a good ground" (Sermon 150, 9). "The one who sows," specifies Augustine elsewhere, "is the Lord; but we are his laborers" (Sermon 72, 3).

Husbandman

The figure of the sower lends itself readily to an expansion into that of the *husbandman* who attends to the various operations necessary to get a good harvest from the land. Commenting again on the parable of the sower, Augustine says:

> It is our concern, whoever we are whom our Lord has appointed as laborers in his field, to say these things to you,

to sow, plant, water, also to dig round trees and manure them. It is our concern to do these things faithfully; yours to receive them faithfully; and our Lord's to help us in our labor, you in your belief, and all who toil but are conquering the world through him (Sermon 101, 4).

We work from the outside, as do the farmers in the field. But were there not One who works from within, the seed would neither sprout nor grow in the field nor would the stalk fill out into a trunk, nor would branches, leaves, or fruit appear (Sermon 152, 1).

Building

Augustine also sees the preacher's work as that of *building* the temple of God. Thus, commenting on Psalm 122:3 (*Jerusalem is built like a city*), he says: "This city, then, is now in course of construction. The stones are being hewn out of the mountains by the hands of the preachers of the truth and being squared off to fit into the everlasting edifice" (*Expositions on the Psalms* 121, 4, 13). And, commenting on Psalm 127:1 (*Unless the Lord build the house, they labor in vain who build it*), he says: "Who are those who labor at the building? All those who preach the word of God in the Church, the ministers of the mysteries" (*Expositions on the Psalms* 126, 2, 37).

Augustine again goes to scripture for a sustained metaphor which is intended to give new and ingenuous expression to the joy brought to souls by the word of God. My soul, says Augustine, "when it has conceived some joy from divine scripture, carries it to term within and endeavors to bring it to birth in your ears and in your soul: prepare within you a nest for the word. For scripture speaks of the turtledove seeking a nest for herself wherein to lay her young" (Sermon 37, 1, 4).

Augustine waxes enthusiastic in his contemplation of the unutterable sublimity of the word of God and of the most exalted and noble mission entrusted to him who is called to proclaim that word. He refers to John's proclamation of it in the opening words of that evangelist's gospel, where John has revealed the "divine and mighty mystery. This beginning of his gospel, John pours forth to us from the source where he himself imbibed it, the heart of the Lord himself. . . . What a great thing is this preaching, forth-telling and foretelling at once. What a great thing to communicate the riches of the heart of the Lord" (Sermon 119, 1-2).

6

God Who Teaches Within

THE EFFICACY OF PREACHING which Augustine has been extolling is not primarily dependent on the personality of the preacher. The preacher is himself, in the final analysis, a disciple of the one and only Master: "United in the same Christian love, we are all hearers of him who is for us in heaven the one and only Master" (*Expositions on the Psalms* 131, 1, 7).

The really operative, stimulating, illuminating, and inspiring power within is the "Word and Master."

> You are doing now what we shall all be doing then. Then indeed there will be no master of the word but the Word and Master. It follows that your duty is to do, ours to admonish; for you are the hearers of the word and we preachers. But within, where none can see, we are all hearers. Within, in the heart, in the hidden recesses of the inner man, where he is teaching you who is prompting you to praise.[1] I speak from the outside, he rouses you from within. All of us, then, inwardly are hearers; and all, outwardly, in the sight of God, must be doers (Sermon 179, 7).

> Go in again, therefore, into your own heart; and, if you are faithful, you will find Christ: it is he indeed who speaks to you. I lift up my voice but he teaches even more effectively in silence. I speak in sounds to be heard; he speaks within by the fear that inspires you. May he then sow my words in

---

1. Probably an allusion to the applause that had just broken out (see Sermon 125, 8; Sermon 301A, 9; Sermon 229E, 4) where laudare has this connotation.

your hearts, now that I have dared to say: Live a good life so
as not to die a bad death. Since there is faith in your hearts,
Christ is there: he will teach you what I am trying to drum
into your ears (Sermon 102, 2).

Augustine draws the same lesson from the words of Christ:
They shall all be taught of God (John 6:45).

Even if they are listening to the voice of a man, yet what
they are understanding comes from within, shines forth
from within, is revealed within. What do men do when they
proclaim from the outside? What am I doing now as I am
speaking? I am simply sending my words out to strike your
ears. If, therefore, he who is within does not reveal what I
have really said what has been the point of my speaking?
The husbandman who cultivates the tree is on the outside;
inside is the Creator (*Homilies on the Gospel of John* 26, 7,
1).

Undoubtedly the most perfect of languages is that which
God speaks in the innermost recesses of the person, without
the intermediary of the human word or even the sacred
scriptures. This is the meaning Augustine sees in the verse of
Genesis that says that *the Lord God had not yet sent rain
upon the earth, nor was there any person to till the soil*
(Genesis 2:5). There were no clouds as yet, those scriptural
figures of the prophets and the apostles, wrapped in the
obscurity of allegories, through whom the rain of truth reaches
man. God was watering his creature "with the inner spring,
speaking to his interior understanding. Man had no need to
receive the rain from the clouds we have mentioned above, for
he was quenching his thirst at his own inner spring, that is from
the truth that was gushing forth from his own innermost
recesses." But after the fall, "the soul that henceforth tills the
soil does have need of the rain that comes down from the
clouds, that is of the teaching that comes from human words,
in order to be able, if indeed he can even in this way, to freshen
from his barrenness and become anew a verdant field. It is to
be hoped that he will at least willingly accept from those
clouds the rain of truth" (*On Genesis: A Refutation of the
Manicheans* 2, 5-6).

The word of God, we read at the beginning of one of Augustine's sermons on the gospel of John, is like a teeming fountain. The preacher dips into that fountain as best he can; but the Lord works in the hearts of the hearers to a far greater degree than the words of the preacher sounding in their ears. Augustine agrees that it may seem unduly bold to touch upon such great mysteries as are contained in the scriptural passage he is glossing, but one ought not to despair "of understanding by the gift of God what the Son of God has deigned to reveal to him. For we must believe that he has willed us to understand what he has deigned to say to us. And if we do not succeed, he will, at our prayer, grant us the understanding of that his word, which word he has given us without our prayer" (*Homilies on the Gospel of John* 22, 1)

It is the Lord who puts into the heart of the preacher what he has to say: and it is the same Lord who, dwelling in the faithful, shows them the truth of what is said. "Christ must not be asleep in you, that is all; then at once you will understand that what I say is true." And he goes on to explain that his hearers must listen with faith: "Christ present in your hearts is the faith of Christ" (*Expositions on the Psalms* 120, 7, 29).

"We do the talking but it is God who does the instructing; we do the talking but it is God who does the teaching. It is not indeed the man who is taught by men who is called blessed, rather *the man whom you instruct, O Lord* (Psalm 94:12). We can plant and water, but it takes God to give life to the seed (see 1 Corinthians 3:7-8). The sower and the waterer work from the outside; he who makes the seed grow operates from within" (Sermon 153, 1).

And so the prayer of the preacher must be: "I thank you, O Lord, for you know what I have said or willed to say. At all events, I have fed my fellow servants with the crumbs from your table. Do you, then, feed and nourish within those whom you have regenerated" (Sermon 225, 4).

This thought is recalled at the end of a sermon to the people of Caesarea in the presence of the Donatist Bishop Emeritus, whom Augustine was trying to bring back into unity within the

Church: "You have heard; he has heard. What God has worked in his soul, he himself knows. For we do nothing else than to assail the ear from without; it is he who is mighty to speak within, it is he who preaches peace and does not cease to preach provided he finds a hearing" (Sermon to the People of the Church of Caesarea 9).

PREACHER: INSTRUMENT OF GOD

This conviction that the preacher is an instrument of God is essential to a proper understanding of Augustine's view on the meaning and value of preaching. This conviction is evident in the passage just cited and in many other passages we have previously quoted. Preaching is the "word of God" not only in the sense that it repeats what God has said in the inspired writings, but further in the sense that it is God himself who is speaking really effectively to people in preaching. Indeed he alone can speak effectively to people, by addressing himself to their innermost essence, enlightening their understanding, touching their heart, moving their will.

The preacher is a humble receptacle (*vasculum*) or little basket wherein the faithful find the bread of the divine word: but the one who puts this bread there is God himself (Sermon 126, 8). "The things we say to you, if they are useful to us and to you, come from him; but what comes from men is falsehood" (*Homilies on the Gospel of John* 5, 1, 3).

The instruments may be of a great variety but the real speaker is always the Lord.

> *The God of gods, the Lord, has spoken,* has spoken in many ways. It is he who has spoken by means of the angels, it is he who has spoken through the mouth of the prophets, has spoken with his own mouth, has spoken through the mouth of his apostles. It is he who speaks through my own humble person. But see what he has done: though he speaks on many different occasions, in many fashions, through many instruments, many mouthpieces, yet it is his voice everywhere that rings out, to pierce, to correct, to inspire (*Expositions on the Psalms* 99, 3, 1).

In a passage already cited in part, where the preachers of the truth are compared to the mountains that are the first to receive the light of the sun and then make that light manifest to the plainland below, Augustine speaks out against the Donatists who were appealing to the leaders of their sect. Augustine insists on the thought that it is not from the mountains that the light comes, but from God: "*You who shine forth marvelously from the everlasting mountains* (Psalm 76:4). With good reason and in solemn tones is here said *you*, lest anyone might think that it is the mountains that are giving him light. . . . Why do they ascribe salvation to humans rather than to God? O human being, the light comes to you indeed by means of the mountain; but it is God who lightens and not the mountains" (*Expositions on the Psalms* 75, 7, 14).

There is a deep theological reason at the root of God's choice of human instruments to communicate his word to people. It is encompassed within the economy of the incarnation. People, says Augustine, were not in a position to read the "Word of God," that Word that is *with God* (John 1:1), too high for human lowliness. Therefore the Word of God himself "came in the flesh, without ever separating himself from the divinity." This in turn, as we know from Saint Paul, led to God choosing in his wisdom *to save all who would believe by the "simple-mindedness" of the gospel message* (1 Corinthians 1:21). "And to preach that gospel message to them, God chose mortal instruments, persons mortal and foredoomed to die. He made use of a mortal tongue to produce mortal sounds, adapted himself to the requirements of mortals by using mortal instruments; and in this he made himself your heaven, that in mortal form you might know the immortal Word and might even yourself become immortal by the participation of that same Word" (*Expositions on the Psalms* 103, sermon 1, 8, 27).

Preaching, that essential ministry of the Church, is but one instance of a typical characteristic of the entire salvific action performed in the Church, wherein human beings are called to communicate to human beings truth and grace.

THE GRACE OF GOD

The preacher is but an instrument. It is God himself who is the real operative agent, working through and by means of the preacher, in the preacher himself and in his hearers. This vision of the preaching mission is at once an incitement to humility and a reminder of the responsibility of this office. It is also a source of encouragement, for the preacher can put his trust in God, inspirer and inner master of speaker and hearer alike.

To the ministry of preaching, Augustine applies the doctrine on the necessity and efficacy of grace which had always been in his mind, from his meditations on scripture, but which gradually became more and more clear to him in the course of the twenty-year controversy with the Pelagians, who denied the necessity and even the existence of grace.

Therefore, Augustine's sermons often begin with the expression of the hope that God will aid the speaker and with an injunction to the faithful to pray to obtain divine grace. "The Holy Spirit teaches us what we ought to say at this moment. We are indeed preparing to speak in praise of Cyprian, the most glorious martyr, whose birthday into heaven we are, as you know, celebrating today" (Sermon 310, 1). "In the first place, I commend to your prayers my weakness, *so that,* as the Apostle says, *the word may be given to me when I open my mouth* (Ephesians 6:19), that I may speak to you in such a way that my speaking may not be dangerous for me and the hearing of me may be salutary for you" (*Expositions on the Psalms* 31, sermon 1, 6). "May the Lord our God assist us, grant us to fulfill as much as we have promised" (*Homilies on the Gospel of John* 9, 1, 1).

The same thought recurs at the end of the sermon, here expressed in the form of thanksgiving. "Let our soul bless the Lord, O my brethren, for he has deigned to give me the ability to speak and you attentiveness and good will" (*Expositions on the Psalms* 103, sermon 4, 19, 15).

Augustine always has special recourse to divine assistance on those occasions when he has to preach about specially important or difficult questions. "What, then, does it mean *to hear the voice of praise* (Psalm 26:7)? I shall tell you if I can manage it, with the aid of the Lord's mercy and of your prayers" (*Expositions on the Psalms* 25, 11, 8). After quoting the scriptural text: *I am the God of Abraham and the God of Isaac and the God of Jacob* (Exodus 3:6-15), Augustine exclaims: "A mighty mystery, this! The Lord is mighty, nonetheless, to open my mouth and your hearts, that I may be able to explain what he has deigned to reveal and you may be able to comprehend to the extent that it is profitable to you" (*Homilies on the Gospel of John* 11, 7, 13). Why did Isaac maintain that he could give but one blessing? (Genesis 27:37). "The Spirit will assist me that I may tell and you may grasp it" (Sermon 4, 24). "Be attentive, beloved! The Lord assist both my will and your expectancy, that I may be able to say what I want to say and as I want to say it" (Sermon 43, 5). "What does it mean to wish, out of pride, to be like God? What do we think motivated that captive to cry out: *Lord, who is like you* (Psalm 71:19)? What is this mismatched likeness? Hear and understand if you can. We believe that he who has set us here to say these words will likewise grant to you the ability to understand" (*Expositions on the Psalms* 70, sermon 2, 6, 23).

When faced, in the course of his sermon, with a specially difficult passage of scripture that has to be explained, Augustine often asks his congregation not only for their attention but also for their prayers. "Observe closely, brethren, be attentive! Aid me with your devout attention, with your unsullied prayers; aid me so that in his name we may get safely out of these narrows" (Sermon 24, 4).

On one occasion, he had to deal with a very far-reaching point, sufficient in itself, he says, to refute the Donatists' thesis. But it was already late: "I have told you this, dear Christians, to make you attentive, as I am in the habit of doing; and at the same time so that you will pray for yourselves and for me, that the Lord may grant me to speak to you as I ought and you to grasp as you ought what I say" (*Homilies on the Gospel of John* 4, 16, 3).

Before commenting on the words of John the Baptist: *This my joy is now complete* (John 3:29), Augustine remarks: "Let us see what follows: it is somewhat difficult to understand. But the same John has said: *A man can receive nothing at all unless it is given him from heaven* (John 3:27), so, when we do not succeed in understanding, let us pray to him who gives from heaven. We are men and can receive nothing at all unless it is given by him who is more than man" (*Homilies on the Gospel of John* 14, 2, 38).

In explanation of Jesus' statement: *I and the Father are one* (John 10:30), Augustine uses the expression: "We are of one substance only." But then he wonders if his hearers have grasped this technical terminology. "You may be having difficulty in understanding what 'of one substance only' means. Let us make a real effort to understand. May God aid me who speaks and you who listen: me, to tell you what is true and suited to you; you, to believe first and foremost, and then to understand according to your abilities" (Sermon 139, 2).

Augustine speaks in the same vein while commenting on the other words of Jesus: "The Father who sent me has commanded me what to say and what to speak. And I know that what he commands means eternal life" (*Homilies on the Gospel of John* 12, 49). "Oh, if he will but grant me to say what I want to say! I am caught in the crossfire of my own poverty and his riches" (Sermon 140, 3).

Augustine refers to the mystery of the Trinity the words spoken by the Father at Jesus' baptism: "*This is my Son* (Matthew 3:17). Where is the undivided Trinity? God has made use of me to render you attentive. Pray for me, and open the womb of your soul; he will himself grant that it shall be filled. Labor together with me. You see what an assignment I have taken on and what are my powers" (Sermon 52, 3). And later in the same sermon: "The Lord will help us. I see that he is helping us. I understand that he is helping us because you are grasping my drift. Your voices show me that you have somewhat understood. I trust that he will help us so that you will understand fully" (Sermon 52, 20). And the sermon concludes with the injunction to pray so that they may understand even what he, the preacher, wanted to say and did not (Sermon 52, 23).

PRAYER WITHIN THE HOMILY

A mention of prayer opens and closes a sermon devoted to the difficult question of achieving a concordance between the genealogies of Matthew and Luke: "When we promised you to treat of this matter, we begged God's help; and if we are now fulfilling our promise, it is by the gift of God" (Sermon 51, 1). And the conclusion of the sermon:

> If there be more to be said about these mysterious treasures, others can investigate them who are more diligent and more worthy. As for me, I have said what I could, with the aid and grace granted me by the Lord, taking account of the limitations of time. If any of you is capable of receiving still more, let him knock at the door of him from whom we too derive all that we are able to say (Sermon 51, 35).

Augustine likewise expresses his hope in God's grace in his treatment of apparent contradictions between two gospel texts (John 16:24 and Luke 10:17-20):

> What has been said we have all heard, but I think not all have understood. This, then, is a summons for you to seek with me, to ask with me, to knock with me, so as to receive. The grace of the Lord will, as we hope, assist us. . . . So let us ask, seek, knock. We are impelled by a devotion animated by faith, not a worldly restlessness but rather an inner submissiveness, that he who sees us knocking will open to us (Sermon 145, 1).

Augustine sees an extremely difficult problem in the passage where Jesus says: *Whoever speaks against the Holy Spirit shall not be forgiven whether in this world or in the world to come* (Matthew 12:32). He begins his long sermon on this text with a confession of his own inadequacy, followed by a profession of trust in the Lord and an injunction to the faithful to aid him with their prayers:

> It is a hard question that emerges from the gospel passage that has just been read. For our own part, we are unable to resolve it; but our ability comes from God (2 Corinthians

3:5), from his aid, as we can receive or take hold of that assistance. First of all, then, realize just how hard the question is; and, seeing the burden that is weighing on my shoulders, pray that my labor may be fruitful. In the aid that will be granted me, you will find strength for your souls (Sermon 171, 1).

And the sermon ends on the same note of humble trust and thanksgiving to the Lord:

I have treated this most difficult question as best I could; and if I have been able to treat it at all, it is by the mercy and aid of the Lord. As for what I have not been able to catch in this exposition of so hard a question, do not blame the Truth for that; for the Truth, even when it hides itself, does but put the devout seeker to a healthy test. No, blame my own weakness, which has not managed to see what there was to understand or else has not managed to explain what I had myself grasped. And if I have been able to discover something with my mind and explain it in my words, thanks be to him from whom I have sought, of whom I have asked, at whose door I have knocked, to get the wherewithal to nourish me in my own meditations and to hand them on to you by my words (Sermon 171, 38).

Sometimes, Augustine's difficulty is not in understanding the scripture text himself but rather in making it intelligible to his congregation. But his approach is the same here too: "The reading of the holy gospel (Matthew 11:2-11) has presented us with a question concerning John the Baptist. May the Lord aid us to resolve it for you as he has resolved it for me" (Sermon 66, 1).

On occasion, not content with exhorting the faithful to prayer, Augustine himself breaks out in an impassioned invocation: "*As the Father has life in himself, so he has given to the Son also to have life in himself*(John 5:26). . . . By this little phrase, *in himself,* he wants to tell us something special. This little phrase encloses a mystery. Let us knock, so that it may be opened to us. O Lord, what does it mean, what you have said? Why did you add *in himself?*" (*Homilies on the Gospel of John* 22, 9, 2).

Another sermon ends with a prayer to Christ, after a quotation of John 14:3: "O Lord Jesus! How is it that you are going to prepare a place, if there are already many rooms in your Father's house, where your own will dwell with you together? Oh, if you take them to yourself, how is it that you come again, if you go not away?" And because these matters cannot be treated summarily, Augustine postpones their treatment to another sermon (*Homilies on the Gospel of John* 67, 4).

Trust in the divine assistance does not dispense the preacher from using whatever devices he considers suited to get out of the dilemma. Thus, on one occasion, Augustine prefers to postpone the interpretation of one passage, in the hope that the explanation of the sequel will serve to clear up the troublesome passage as well:

> *The Father is no man's judge: he has put judgment entirely into the Son's hands* (John 5:22). For the moment the questions raised leave us perplexed. The Lord will see to it that we shall be contented by a solution being found. So it is, brethren: no question could give cause for joy upon its solution, did it not call for exertion upon its presentation. May the Lord, then, walk with us: perhaps what follows will help to make things clear, to some extent. His light has been hidden by clouds; and it is no easy matter to soar like the eagle up above all the clouds that cover the whole earth (see Sirach 24:6), so as to see sheer pure light in the words of the Lord. Now, therefore, let us postpone this hard question and see what comes next, in the expectation that he will pierce our gloom with the warmth of his rays and deign to make himself somewhat clearer in what follows (*Homilies on the Gospel of John* 19, 5, 14).

There are, however, some cases in which the hard questions simply cannot be passed over without disappointment and even frustrating the congregation. Then the only recourse is to prayer:

> There is still another question here involved. I believe it would be an assignment beyond my powers, the limitations of time and your own capacities, to present a thorough treatment of its every most intricate aspect and to clarify each as it deserves. Yet, seeing that your expectation does not allow me to pass on to other matters without at least saying something on this point, take what I can give you.

And if I do not manage to live up to your expectations, ask
the rest from him who hs sent us to plant and water (1 Corinthians 3:6 — *Homilies on the Gospel of John* 53, 4, 1).

Augustine finds in his own personal experience the confirmation of that truth that he never tires of instilling into his
hearers: that it is the grace of God that makes effective the
word of him who proclaims God's gospel. He tells us that
when he was once speaking to the people on Christ's promise
that anyone giving a cup of cold water to one of his disciples
would not lose his reward (Matthew 10:42), God aided him
and "from that cold water there leapt up, as it were a *flame* (2
Maccabees 1:32) kindling and warming even the cold hearts
of people to accomplish works of mercy in the hope of the
heavenly reward" (*Christian Instruction* 4, 37).

Even slips and lapses of memory serve, in God's hands, to
make his word fruitful. One day, Augustine lost the thread of
his argument in the course of a sermon and began denouncing
and arguing against the Manicheans, something he had not
intended doing that day and in that context! Accustomed as he
was to discern in every event, great or small, the paternal
providence of the Lord, he spoke to his clergy at table about
this little lapse, which they themselves had noticed; and
Augustine told them that he thought the Lord *in whose hands
we are and all our affairs* (Wisdom 7:16) had arranged things
that way to bring back someone who had gone astray. A day or
two later, there came to the monastery a certain merchant,
Fermus, by name, a staunch Manichean. He wanted to abjure
his error; and when asked, he declared that it had been that
digression of Augustine's in the sermon that had hit him
between the eyes (*Life* 15). It is therefore no surprise to find
Augustine speaking of a "divine inspiration" guiding him in
the choice of subjects (Sermon 180, 4) and in the manner of
treating them (Sermon 93, 2).

Book 4 of Augustine's *Christian Instruction* is devoted to
instructing the preacher how to expound the word of God.
Augustine has enjoined the preacher to make use not only of
the Bible but of the techniques furnished by secular orators
and traditional literary precepts. And at the end, his parting

injunction is prayer, prayer fervent and humble on the part of whoever "labors with word and teaching for the eternal salvation of men and women." Let every preacher pray at the outset of his own sermons, let him pray when he is composing sermons for the use of others, and let him give thanks for good results to the One *in whose hands we are and all our words* (Wisdom 7:16).

THE DEBT OF MINISTRY

The shepherd of souls is under compelling obligation to administer the word of God openhandedly to the faithful: for that word is food, is light, is water, thirst-quenching and life-giving, is medicine, is seed, is, in sum, calculated to satisfy the deepest and most vital needs of the Christian. Augustine is conscious of paying a "debt" when he starts to preach: "I know that I owe it to you, dear Christians; I consider you as my creditors" (Sermon 153, 1). It is a debt that is never paid off in full, being identical with the very mission of the shepherd of souls, as Augustine brings out in the concluding words of one sermon:

> I believe I have spoken enough; yet I have not finished explaining the gospel passage that has been read. Were I to say what still remains to be said, it would be too much for you; and I fear even what you have taken in would spill out again! Be satisfied, therefore, dear Christians, with what has been said. We are debtors, not for the moment only but as long as we live, seeing that we live for you (*Homilies on the Gospel of John* 18, 12, 1).

This is a debt imposed by love. In one of his sermons, explaining the gospel of John, Augustine ran out of time before he had finished his explanation. He excused himself, telling his congregation he would be in their debt (*Homilies on the Gospel of John* 56, 5, 19). His next sermon he began as follows: "I have not forgotten my debt and I agree that it is now time to pay it. May he grant me to pay it who granted me to owe it. He is indeed the donor of that love of which it is said: *Keep out of debt altogether, except that perpetual debt of love which we owe one another* (Romans 13:8); may he give me likewise the words I admit I owe to them I love" (*Homilies on the Gospel of John* 57, 1).

The apostle's admonition is clear: *Preach the word, insistently in season and out of season* (2 Timothy 4:2).

> Judging by these words, we too, insignificant as we are, are seasonable for the well-disposed, unseasonable for the ill-disposed. For the hungry person, the bread offered is seasonable; for the sick person, force-feeding is unseasonable. The one has the food simply put in his or her hands; the other has it forced down his or her throat. To the one the refreshment is welcome, to the other hateful. But love does not abandon either the one or the other (Sermon 299A, 2).

Augustine sees in the words used by God in commissioning Ezekiel as a prophet (Sermon Mai 3, 5-7) a stern warning to shepherds of souls not to hush up bitter truths but rather speak them openly to the people of God: "The words addressed to the prophet are special cause for trembling to us, the leaders whom the Lord has commissioned to speak to his people." Then, after quoting a brief passage from the prophet, Augustine concludes: "If I keep silence, if I hush up, I see myself exposed, I do not say to a great risk merely, but to irremediable ruin" (Sermon 17, 2).

The Letter to the Hebrews likewise reminds the pastor of his duty to speak frankly:

> In all my words, I am holding up a mirror to you. On the other hand, they are not my words; I am speaking on orders from the Lord; I cannot be silent, for he strikes terror into me. Who would not prefer to be silent and not to have to give an account of you? But the fact remains that we have been saddled with a burden that we cannot and must not shake off our shoulders. You have heard, my brethren, when the Letter to the Hebrews was being read: *Obey your rulers and recognize their authority. They are like people standing guard over your spiritual good, and they have great responsibility.* Try to make their work a pleasure and not a burden — by so doing you will help not only them but yourselves (Hebrews 13:17 — Sermon 82, 15).

Augustine sees the will of God, so clearly and openly proclaimed by holy scripture, as being often indicated by daily circumstances. And Augustine is always disposed to accept such signs. Thus, on one occasion, he was on the point of leaving Hippo to set out on one of his journeys when he was prevented by inclement weather. To his congregation he says: "I have been ordered, my dear Christians, to speak to you about this psalm and I have had no choice but to obey. The Lord has willed, you see, to hold up my departure by these torrential rains; thus has he ordered me not to spare my tongue with you; as far as the heart is concerned, you are always with me, as I with you" (*Expositions on the Psalms* 36, sermon 2, 1, 1).

Conscious as he is of his own responsibility, the preacher does not hesitate to admonish his hearers that they in turn must render an account of their doings to God.

> We do not flatter you. Put not your hope in us. Even as we do not flatter ourselves, no more do we flatter you: let each bear his own burden. Upon us falls the duty of speaking, so as not to be judged and condemned; on you falls the duty of listening, of listening with your heart, so as not to be called to account in respect of what we give you: or, better, so as to be able to show a profit and not a loss when you are so called to account (*Homilies on the Gospel of John* 12, 4, 39).

> Watch how you believe, watch how you receive (the word): after the preacher comes the judge; after the one who dispenses comes the one who demands a return (*Expositions on the Psalms* 103, sermon 1, 11, 67).

> We scare you because we are ourselves afraid. Show us that we have no reason to be afraid and we will stop frightening you. But God himself teaches us to fear; and that outweighs the word of any person telling us not to fear. Indeed, *everyone was afraid, and they proclaimed the works of God* (Psalm 64:9). May God be able to number us among those who have feared and have proclaimed. Because we fear, we proclaim to you the message, brethren (*Expositions on the Psalms* 63, 19, 21).

Terrified at his responsibility before the God who sent him, the preacher proclaims his own freedom in regard to the faithful:

> You all know that we are going to have to render an account of the bread we have received and are distributing. You

know that full well, dear Christians. The pages of Holy Writ are not silent, God does not flatter us. You can remark the freedom we use toward you in speaking to you from this place. And if ever I myself or anyone speaking to you from this place is wanting in freedom, God's own word certainly has fear of no one. As for us, whether because we fear or because we are free, we are obliged to proclaim him who fears no one. This is the grace that has been given you by God and not by mortals: that even through the mouths of the fearful you should hear him who is free (*Expositions on the Psalms* 103, sermon 1, 19, 13).

Were the bishop to be silent, the faithful could accuse him and put the blame on him for his silence: "From this high place, I have been admonishing, proclaiming, announcing, spelling out right up till now the chastisements awaiting drunkards. You cannot say: 'I never heard! The Lord will demand an accounting of my soul from him, because he kept silent' " (Sermon 151, 4).

The bishop is convinced that his own responsibility to preach what the Lord wants him to preach in the way the Lord wants him to preach it — that this responsibility is much graver than that incumbent upon his hearers. "I have shown you, my dear and well-beloved Christians, as well as I was able and with the aid the Lord deigned to give me, how much safer you are in your position as listeners than we in our position as preachers" (Sermon 179, 7). "Dangerous is the office of master; safe is the status of disciple. . . . He is in a safer position who listens to the word than is he who proffers it. . . . It is safer if both we who speak and you who listen know ourselves to be fellow-disciples in the school of the one and only Master" (Sermon 23, 1-2). "We are not so devoid of human feelings and of the sound thoughts suggested by faith, as not to realize the dangers we are running, we who preach to the people the word of God. We are consoled by the certainty that your prayers are profitable to us in the dangers inherent in our ministry. Do you want to know, brethren, how much more secure your position is than ours? I shall cite you another word of the same apostle, which says: *Let every one of you be quick to listen but slow to speak* (James 1:19)" (Sermon 179, 1).

His awareness of his own responsibility suggests to the preacher the subjects he must treat, and these are not those most welcome to the hearers. Rather, they are the ones that need most to be spoken about, especially if there are abuses to be corrected. On his way through Bulla Regia, Augustine is invited by the local bishop to speak to the people. Dom Morin introduces this sermon with the comment: "Augustine shows amazing and truly evangelical strength of character in lashing out at the disorders to which the people of this town were abandoning themselves, prostitution and worldly spectacles."[2] And here is how Augustine did speak, near the end of his sermon:

> I would not have said these things to you, had I heard you well spoken of. But had I kept silent I fear I would be judged together with you. God, therefore, willed, my brethren, that I should be passing through here. My brother detained me, commanding, constraining, and imploring me to speak to you. Of what should I then have spoken if not of what frightens me most? Of what if not of that which saddens me most? Do you know that I and you alike are going to have to render the strictest accounting to God of your plaudits? Do you think that these plaudits honor me? They are not an honor, but a burden to me. They will cost me a strict accounting. I fear greatly that Christ in his judgment seat will say to us: "Wicked servants, you accepted willingly the plaudits of my people and you concealed from them in silence the death (that was threatening them)" (Sermon 306B, 9).

When Augustine is speaking of detachment from temporal goods, he says in reply to those claiming themselves to be in legitimate possession of their own holdings: "I give you this warning, brethren, and I give it to you as a brother. God commands, and I admonish, being myself in turn admonished. I am terrified of him who will not let me keep silence. He demands of me what he has given me, for he has given it to me to use for good and not to keep to myself" (Sermon 125, 8).

---

2. Miscellanea Agostiniana I, page 80.

Still more urgent, no doubt because of the greater urgency of the problem, are Augustine's words in recalling his hearers to loyalty to the marriage bond and to generally proper behavior in the whole realm of sex. He is the more insistent because he is compelled bitterly to admit that he has been getting nowhere in the past on this point: "Look, you, I tell it to you, I shout it at you, to satisfy my obligation. God sends me to bestow, not to exact. Yet where possible, where practicable, where permissible, where feasible, we do rebuke, we do reprove, we do launch anathemas and excommunications: and with it all we do not succeed in bringing you into line" (Sermon 224, 3).

Augustine, like many other fathers of the Church, was dead set against the abuse of unnecessary and gratuitous swearing of oaths; he even felt obliged to take drastic measures in this regard with his clergy who lived together with him in the bishop's quarters (*Life* 25). At the end of one sermon in which he had castigated this abuse, admitting the while that he had himself been a victim of this "most baneful and deadly custom" (Sermon 180, 10), the bishop declares that he had several times shied away from treating this subject: "I feared that I would have rendered those who would not have listened to me more culpable by my admonitions and prohibitions; but today another fear has got the upper hand in me, the fear of refusing to say what I was being ordered to say" (Sermon 180, 14).

Augustine professes himself a debtor even to those who are far off, those who are outside the Church entirely. Whether or not they are disposed to listen to the word of truth, he must at least make the effort to bring it to them. These hearers may indeed bear no fruit, but the reward of God will not be wanting. Thus does Augustine reply to the Donatist Cresconius, who had said it was pointless for Catholics to be insistent in inducing schismatics to come back to the unity of the Church:

> The faithful preacher of justice will not be deprived of the reward of his labor by the Lord, even though he may be rejected by human beings. We are doing a sure thing while aiming at an unsure thing. The unsure thing, I repeat, is the soul of the hearer, not the reward of the speaker. We are not

sure that the ones to whom we preach the truth will assent to it, but we are sure that the truth must be preached to them too; and we are sure that the reward due the faithful preacher is laid up for him, whether he be heard or scorned, or even has to suffer all manner of temporal adversity for this his preaching (*Answer to Cresconius* 1, 7).

And Augustine appeals to the example of Christ himself, who preached and proclaimed the truth not only to the disciples and the well-disposed crowds, but even to his obstinate enemies, despite the fact that he knew that it would not help them to salvation.

But it may be that he desired, by his example, to give strength to us who cannot foresee whether men and women are going to believe or not. Thus, let us not lose heart because we have spoken to the hard-hearted and the totally perverse, spoken to them to no purpose so far as their salvation is concerned. Let us not desist, tired of our fruitless labor, from preaching the gospel. Let us go on doing that at all costs (*Answer to Cresconius* 1, 10).

No danger, not even the danger of death itself, ought to induce the faithful servant of the Lord to be silent in the face of adversaries and persecutors. Augustine appeals to the example of Saint Cyprian:

The Blessed Cyprian had no fear of the demon worshippers, nor ought we to fear the cliques of the heretics, nor the gangs of the presumptuous pagan baiters and martyrdom seekers. Only let us pray heartily to the Lord that no one may induce us to keep silent. And if they kill us for our faith, we say: Thanks be to God! And if they do not kill us, how much longer shall we have to live down here? Even if we reach extreme old age, what matter? Are we not going to have to die one day? Ought the ministry of our heart and of our tongue ever fall silent in the few brief days of this life of ours here on earth? Never! (Sermon 313E, 7).

7

The Divine and Human Elements

AUGUSTINE COULD NOT FAIL to advert to the dual element, human and divine, involved in the Christian priesthood. His precise treatment of this constant duality is of obvious interest from the point of doctrine, and it also has specially interesting consequences on the plane of the practical pastorate. We have therefore thought it opportune to deal with it here, since our avowed purpose is to study the thought of Augustine on the priesthood as that thought provides guidance and assistance for the present day shepherd of souls.

Augustine's personal temperamental inclination was to delve deeply into the transcendent reality, the spiritual substratum of any element of doctrine or religious practice. This inclination had been reinforced by his familiarity with Platonic thought, especially as mediated by the Neoplatonism of Plotinus and Porphyry. Platonism, especially this variety, tended to see in the sensible world a mere shadow of the spiritual reality and to insist that the fullness of genuine truth was present only in that transcendent spiritual dimension. Moreover, Augustine was animated by an unaffected and unswerving longing for a union with God that would bypass entirely the mediating agency of any creature. This deep-seated religious desire could easily lead him to relegate to the lowest level those sensible aspects wherein the inexhaustible wealth of the transcendent God is concealed, out of conde-scension toward human fragility.

Yet no man can be so totally absorbed by the world of the spirit as to close his eyes entirely to the sensible world in which he is living his daily life. We must therefore examine

Augustine's feelings on this matter from the moment when the will of God, as manifested by the voice of the people of Hippo confirmed by the bishop, called him to devote his life to the priestly and later the episcopal ministry.

He was in daily contact with his flock, and the varied needs of that flock were not always such as could be easily integrated into a purely and exclusively religious context. This could not fail to draw his attention, as shepherd of souls, to certain aspects of religious truth and life which would, in all probability, have remained outside the scope of his interests, had he remained the scholar and ascetic in the industrious seclusion of the monastery at Thagaste.

Augustine was therefore temperamentally inclined and impelled by his pastoral obligations to reflect deeply on the dual aspect, exterior and interior, human and divine, that is characteristic of the priesthood. Soon a further factor came into play to stimulate still further reflection: the Donatists were claiming that the effectiveness of the sacraments was dependent on the holiness of the minister. This posed an urgent problem of clarification. A very clear distinction had to be drawn between the obviously transcendent nature and source of the powers belonging to the priest on the one hand and that priest's human behavior, whether righteous or sinful, on the other.

And even apart from any polemical concern, Augustine would have been compelled to face this whole problem in the interests of the enlightenment and consolation of the minds of the faithful, upset by the distinctly less than edifying conduct of some pastors. And this concern with the scandal of the faithful is our best starting point in any consideration of Augustine's thought and writing on this topic.

SCANDALOUS BEHAVIOR OF PASTORS

A certain Felicia, a virgin consecrated to God, had written to Augustine (a letter which has not come down to us), expressing her pained surprise at the scandalous behavior of certain pastors of souls and confessing that this had constituted a serious temptation against faith for her. This was all the more serious in her case since she was (as appears from Augustine's letter to her in reply) a recent convert from the Donatist schism, on whom considerable effort had had to be expended and considerable pressure brought to bear to make her come back to the unity of the Catholic Church. Augustine sees clearly that she must be fully enlightened on this difficult question.

The crucial distinction, as Augustine sees (and expresses) it, is that between the priest's mission and his personal conduct. In the former, Christ himself is working for the salvation and sanctification of souls; in the latter the priest is acting as a mere human individual who will have to answer for his deeds at the moment of final separation of the righteous from the wicked. But personal misconduct does not invalidate the exercise of the priest's sacerdotal functions nor does it in any way compromise their effectiveness. Even in the preaching mission, the Christian must simply learn to distinguish between the truth being proclaimed and the consistency or inconsistency of the preacher's own conduct with what he is saying.

It is understandable, begins Augustine in his letter to Felicia, that the faithful should be upset by the weaknesses or outright wickedness of their fellowmen and fellow Christians. Saint Paul found it hard to take (2 Corinthians 11:29) and so does he himself, says Augustine. For that very reason he is writing to console and encourage Felicia.

The main theme and motif of his letter are expressed almost in passing but it reflects the very crux of Augustine's ecclesiology (an ecclesiology reiterated in the Constitution *Lumen gentium*, which bases the whole doctrine concerning the Church on that "mystery" dimension present in its first chapter).

Augustine, then, tells Felicia he is writing to her out of concern for her salvation "because in the body of our Lord Jesus Christ, which is his Church and the unity of its members, you have become in very truth blood kin to us, beloved as a member worthy of honor in the Christian fellowship, and you live together with us in his Holy Spirit" (Letter 208, 1).

Augustine's thought as here expressed may fairly well be developed as follows, in the light of his overall ecclesiology. There is a mystery of grace into which the Christian has entered by the ministry of the priest but whose power ultimately derives from Christ and his Spirit.

Christ himself predicted the scandals that would come in the Church (Matthew 18:7), so that we should not waver in our faith when we encounter them. And Augustine interprets Christ's prophecy in the light of a Pauline text referring more specifically to the shepherds of Christ's flock: "Who are these men if not those of whom the Apostle says: *Who seek their own interests and not those of Jesus Christ* (Philippians 2:21). There are therefore some men who use their pastoral office to look after Christ's flock; but there are others whose only thought, in that office, is for their own temporal honor and worldly advantage."

With all the wisdom of his seventy years,[1] Augustine flatly warns against naive optimism. Experience and God's own work speak against it. What happened in the days of Saint Paul, what is happening now, will always be occurring in the Church. "Individuals of both sorts will come and go, but it is inevitable that these two types of pastors will always be present in the Catholic Church itself, right down to the end of the world and Christ's last judgment" (Letter 208, 2).

There is no contradiction between this sort of statement and the words spoken by Augustine in 412 in a sermon in Carthage, on the occasion of the consecration of a new bishop: "What shall we say then, Are there bad bishops? No, there are not. I venture to say with absolute certainty, there are no bad bishops; because if they are bad, they are not bishops" (Sermon 340A, 6). As Augustine has said just a few minutes previously in that same sermon, such a man "is bishop in name

---

1. This would be Augustine's age at the time of writing this letter, if, as the Maurists suspect, the letter is to be linked to the scandalous conduct of Anthony, the young bishop of Fussala, of which he speaks in his Letter 209 to Pope Saint Celestine.

but not in fact; his is an empty title." Augustine uses an arresting comparison to bring out his point: a beggar may go by the name of Happy (Felix) and yet be no less unhappy for that reason!

Moreover, continues Augustine in his letter to Felicia, it is the same with the sheep as with the shepherds: "Even as there are good and wicked shepherds, so too within the flock there are the good and the bad. The good are called lambs and the bad goats." And Augustine then proceeds to make a point, based on the gospel texts and other scriptural passages, which he never tires of making, especially in his arguments against the Donatists. This state of affairs within the Church will continue till the end of the world; men and women cannot effect that separation that God has reserved to himself at the end of the time. Sheep and goats "are mingled and pasture together, until the Chief of Shepherds (1 Peter 5:4) shall come and separate the sheep from the goats, as he has promised (Matthew 25:32). He has indeed enjoined upon us union, reserving to himself separation, for the business of separating belongs to him who cannot be mistaken" (Letter 208, 3).

From this Augustine derives a motivation for persevering in unity, undaunted by any scandals:

> It is our Chief Shepherd himself who has warned us, when he speaks in the gospel of the good shepherds, to refrain from putting our trust even in them, to refrain from setting our hopes on them because of their good works; rather, he tells us, we ought to give glory to him who has made them so, to the Father who is in heaven (Matthew 5:16). And as for the wicked shepherds, that same Chief Shepherd warns the sheep that they must do what these wicked shepherds teach but not what they do (Matthew 23:3).

In thus following the good teaching of even the wicked shepherds, those good teachings that come from Christ himself, "the sheep pasture in safety, for even under wicked shepherds they are nourished by the fodder of the Lord" (Letter 208, 4).

Even when the sheep are imitating the good actions of the pastors and shepherds, adds Augustine, they must not "put their hope in him by whose ministry they have been brought into the flock, but rather in the Lord by whose blood they have been bought" (Letter 208, 6). Let Felicia, then, love the Lord and his Church with all her heart. That is what really matters.

To reject the Church because there are some unworthy persons even within her higher ranks would be ruinous, because it is in the Church that the faithful find Christ, the Savior, but it would be idiotic to put one's trust in humans rather than in Christ.

Augustine asks in one sermon: "What, then, if the people should meet with a bad bishop? Our Lord, the Bishop of bishops,[2] has made sure that your hope should not depend on any human being" (Sermon 340A, 8). And a little later in the same sermon comes the famous injunction: "Whatever we are like, your hope must not be in us . . . your hope must not be in us, your hope must not be in humanity. Whether good or bad, we are servants" (Sermon 340A, 9).

When he thus speaks of "wicked shepherds" who are guilty of scandalizing the faithful, Augustine has in mind those who consciously and deliberately put their own interests before the good of souls, as we have already heard him say and as he is fond of repeating; he is thinking of the bishop "who rejoices in that honor rather than the salvation of God's flock, who in that high office seeks his own ends, not those of Jesus Christ" (Sermon 340A, 4).

The "wicked shepherds" are "those who feed Christ's sheep with the desire to make them their own instead of Christ's . . . are proved guilty of loving themselves and not Christ; by a passion for boasting, ruling, or acquiring possessions, instead of a love of obeying, helping, and pleasing God" (*Homilies on the Gospel of John* 123, 58).

These are the ones who "love to hear themselves called by the name of pastors but are unwilling to discharge the duties of pastors," who "pasture themselves and not the sheep," in

---

2. Saint Maximus of Turin likewise calls Christ "Bishop of bishops" (Sermon 79, 18).

defiance of the plain fact that "you are given leaders whose duty it is to care for those they lead, and by no means to seek their own advantage from their position as leader but that of those they serve" (Sermon 46, 1-2). Or again, they are the ones who "preach the gospel as opportunity occurs, seeking their own advantage from others, whether pecuniary reward, honors, or human praise" (Sermon 137, 5).

Such are the unworthy pastors, all of them deserving of severe condemnation. But Augustine is not unaware of or unattentive to the fact that all are sinners, even priests and himself first of all, at least out of human weakness (see Letter 265, 8).

THE SINFULNESS OF PASTORS

Citing the warning in Leviticus: *First offer sacrifices for your own sins and then for the people* (Leviticus 16:6; see Hebrews 7:26), he asks: "But may it be that the priests of the people of old were sinners while those of the new people are not?" And his immediate vigorous retort is: "Indeed, my brethren, because God has willed it, I am his priest: and with you I beat my breast, with you I crave pardon, with you I hope in the mercy of God." The apostles themselves were sinners, for they too prayed daily, in fulfillment of the Lord's command, to obtain pardon of their sins (Sermon 137, 5).

Augustine's forthrightness in denouncing the disorders of some churchmen ought not to make us think the whole clergy was corrupt. In a work composed when he was not yet ordained, Augustine could declare:

> How many men of the finest and most holy (optimos viros sanctissimosque) have I come to know among the bishops, how many among the priests, how many among the deacons and in every rank of the ministers of the divine mysteries. Their virtue seems to me all the more worthy of admiration and praise considering how much harder it is to practice in the most dissimilar environments and in a way of life that is anything but placid. For their charges are not sound and healthy men but such as need constant care and attention.

They must have patience with the common vices in order to cure them and must swear out the plague until they can mitigate it. It is a very hard thing in such an environment to keep personal conduct above reproach and to preserve an even and tranquil state of mind (*The Morals of the Catholic Church* 32, 69).

One special danger always incurred by the ministers of the altar, mere men that they are and yet called to teach the things of God, is the temptation to pride, a temptation not unknown to Saint Paul (Letter 266, 2-3) and all the more frequent because it is so easy to find servile flatterers motivated by self-interest (Sermon 340A, 2).

Every Christian is, of course, exposed to a great number and variety of temptations, but the storms threatening the Church are the special trials of the steersman who is managing the ship. And these trials are the more serious, the higher the post a man occupies in the Church (*Expositions on the Psalms* 106, 7).

Augustine is equally firm in his insistence on the necessity of every faithful Christian avoiding two opposite extremes: leaving the Church because of the scandal provoked by wicked pastors, and putting his trust in good pastors. To the passages already cited in this regard we can add several others and we think this quite worthwhile since this is an absolutely basic tenet of Augustine, applicable to clergy and laity alike.

PRIESTLY MINISTRY

Christ is the gateway to the city of God; "therefore he who preaches in the gate, let him say: 'Put not your trust in me; enter not by me but by the gate' " (*Expositions on the Psalms* 126, 13, 9).

"The whole of our hope is set in Christ." Thus does Augustine begin a long sermon on Ezekiel 34. In this sermon he lashes out at the false shepherds who seek only their own advantage and proposes the ideal of the true shepherd who sacrifices himself for the flock (Sermon 46).

In like manner, at the beginning of another sermon centered on the Johannine figure of the Good Shepherd (John 10:1-16), Augustine recalls "your Master in heaven, in whom you have put your hope" (Sermon 137, 1). Later in this sermon, he counsels that whoever listens to the message of salvation proclaimed by one whose own fault prevents him from enjoying that salvation himself will nonetheless benefit if he puts his hope in the One from whom the salvation comes, whereas the preacher will reap nothing but harm from the message (Sermon 137, 5).

"The man desirous of baptism ought not to put his hope in the man who is the minister. Rather he ought to draw near in solid confidence to Christ himself, as to the immutable source, the ineradicable root, the indestructible head" (*Against the Letter of Petilian* 3, 52, 64).

On the other hand, the absolute primacy of the operation of Christ, as source, root, and head, ought not to lead anyone to forget that the ministerial action of the priest is necessary for the faithful; without him they are going to be left without the spiritual nourishment indispensable to them and be exposed, defenseless, to the peril of everlasting death. This whole theme is extensively developed in Letter 238, in which Augustine goes into great detail on the duties of the ministers of the altar to their congregations in the face of the dangers of the barbarian invasion. We have already reported several passages from that letter which are specially pertinent to this point and we shall speak of it again in our last chapter.

Commenting on the order given by Christ to the lepers to present themselves to the priests (Luke 17:14), Augustine links it with the sending of Paul to Ananias (Acts 9:7-19) and says: "He was sent to Ananias to receive from that priesthood constituted in the Church the mystery of the doctrine of faith." And Augustine goes on to speak of the reason for the necessity of such a ministry. Here he seems to want to forestall the objection that it might seem to set a limit to the divine omnipotence. Augustine is quite outspoken:

> Not that the Lord cannot do everything by himself — is
> there indeed, even in the Church, anyone else but the Lord
> himself who effects such things? — but so that the common
> fellowship of the faithful may present, so to speak, one
> single color, that of the truth [whereas leprosy blotches a
> healthy skin], with approval being given by one group to
> what is done by the other, and with the doctrine of the true
> faith being mutually communicated in all that is expressed
> by words or signified by sacraments (*Questions on the
> Gospel* 2, 40).

In other words, the priestly ministry is for the good of the
Church, so that the Church may not be entirely passive in the
work of salvation, so that its members may not be isolated but
rather may cooperate effectively, in fraternal solidarity, with
the action of God.

Word and *sacrament* are the two indispensable forms of
assistance owed by the priest to the faithful. In both ministries,
the divine and the human element are intimately associated.
The truth which the preacher proclaims in his preaching is
from God and revealed by God; but it is the human preacher
who proclaims that truth, using the powers of his own mind
and the commitment of his own heart. The sacrament which
the priest distributes is from God and instituted by Christ as a
channel of his grace, but there is need for the action of the
priest in order that the sacrament and its power shall be
communicated to the faithful.

We can, indeed, speak in a broad sense of a divine element
in the mission of the priest as such, inasmuch as he is a priest
(as Augustine says of himself), "by God's gracious decree"
(Sermon 355, 2). The ultimate reason for any priest being a
priest is that "the servant ought not to gainsay the master"
(*Ibid.*). And Augustine recalls in the *Confessions* that it was
God who had "led and brought" him by promptings and dire
warnings, by consolations and injunctions, "to preach his
word and dispense his mystery to the people."

Two points thus emerge clearly, each vitally complementary
to the other. On the one hand, the work of salvation is a divine
operation. Surely no one has asserted as vigorously as
Augustine the absolute primacy, the irrevocable and incontro-

vertible necessity of the divine initiative in everything related to the economy of salvation: suffice it to recall the guiding principles of Augustine's whole anti-Pelagian polemic and of his entire theology of grace and predestination. On the other hand, Augustine obviously holds it to be equally patent that man is called to work for the salvation of man and that this assignment pertains, in absolutely privileged and necessary fashion, to the ministers of the Church.

There are many passages in Augustine where the two elements are strictly correlated, in a way calculated to assert the same synergism between God and man in the life of the Church as that asserted in Augustine's doctrine of grace and freedom.

Consider Augustine's commentary on Psalm 127:

> *Unless the Lord build the house, they labor in vain who build it.* And so it is the Lord who builds the house; it is the Lord Jesus Christ who is building his own house. All labor in the building, but unless he build *they labor in vain who build it.* Who are those who labor at the building? All those who preach the word of God in the Church, the ministers of the mysteries of God. In this present time, we all run, we all labor, we all build. And before our time, too, there were those who ran, those who labored, those who built, but *unless the Lord build the house, they labor in vain who build it.* ... We speak from the outside but he builds within. ... It is he who builds, who admonishes, who strikes terror into your hearts, who opens your mind and directs it to the faith; and yet we too labor as workmen.

And later in the same sermon, Augustine thus explains the office of the bishop as *guardian*:

> We can see your going out and your coming in, but we do not see what you are thinking in your hearts. We cannot, indeed, even see what you are doing in your homes. How, then, are we guardians? After the fashion of humans: to the best of our ability, according to our endowment. Since we, then, guard after the fashion of humans and cannot do it perfectly, shall you therefore remain without a guardian? No, of course not! For where, indeed, is he of whom it is said: *Unless the Lord guard the city, they labor in vain who guard it?* We labor at our guard duties but our labor is in vain unless he guards you who sees your thoughts (*Expositions on the Psalms* 126, 2, 32).

We have mentioned that it was the Donatist danger that prompted Augustine to treat this whole problem of the collaboration of human and divine elements in this work of salvation. The Donatists had made the efficacy of word and sacrament depend on the holiness of the minister. The Donatist Bishop Petilian had objected: "If a man knows the priestly formulae by heart, is he indeed a priest simply because he proclaims these priestly formulae with a sacrilegious mouth?" Augustine's reply is vigorous and trenchant: "For a man to be a true priest, he must be clothed not only with the sacrament but also with righteousness, as it is written: *Your priests clothe themselves with righteousness* (Psalm 132:9). But the man who is a priest 'only in virtue of a sacrament,' " says Augustine, is like "the high priest Caiaphas, persecutor of the one and most true Priest." But Augustine at once adds: "Although he be not true himself, what he dispenses is true if he gives not of his own but what is of God," even as Caiaphas when he prophesied. And he goes on to explain that a distinction must always be made, in the priest as in other people, between his vice which is his own and the truth which is not his own but God's (*Against the Letter of Petilian* 2, 30, 69).

Thus there is in the priest one element that is his own, and purely human, namely sin and all human frailty; but there is also another element that is divine, a truth which he proclaims and which transcends him.

Such a consideration of the ministry of the word can readily and naturally be extended to cover the sacramental ministry as well, as Augustine does in the following passage, in which he counterattacks against Petilian to clarify the status and function of the priestly minister:

How then is that word of Scripture true that says: *The planter and the waterer are nothing compared with God who gives life to the seed* (1 Corinthians 3:7), unless it means that the minister of Christ is significant only with reference to God's purpose? He is something in the order of the administration and dispensation of word and sacrament, but he is nothing in the order of purification and justification. For the only one who works in the inner person is he through whom the whole person was created and who, while remaining God, was made man; this is he of whom it was said *He cleanses their hearts by faith* (Acts 15:9) and again *who justifies the sinful* (Romans 4:5 — *Against the Letter of Petilian* 3, 54, 66).

It follows that "the minister, that is the dispenser of the word and mystery of the gospel, if he be good, is a partner (consocius) of the gospel; if, on the other hand, he be wicked, he does not, for that reason, cease to be a dispenser of the gospel" (*Against the Letter of Petilian* 3, 55, 67).

PRIEST AND SACRIFICE

In the light of all the passages here cited and of Augustine's whole thinking on the Church, we consider Jacques Pintard's conclusion justified. This scholar, after a thorough theological study of Augustine's thought, speaks of the Augustinian conviction of a *sacerdotium visibile invisibilis sacerdotis sacramentum* (visible priesthood as a sacramental sign of the invisible priest).[3] Pintard grants that Augustine did not use this precise formulation, but he feels, rightly we believe, that the notion is a necessary consequence of the intimate connection between *sacerdos* (priest) and *sacrificium* (sacrifice).

Pintard has an excellent summary of the practical consequences deduced by Augustine from the relationship between the hierarchical priesthood and the High Priest, Jesus Christ. These consequences can all be expressed simply in the fact that the one who has received the sacrament of orders ought to radiate Christian love, so as to be conformed to the Shepherd of shepherds.[4] We might here mention some other consequences

3. *Le sacerdoce selon Saint Augustin,* 1960, page 387 (cited in note 15, Chapter 2).

4. *Ibid.,* pages 387-392.

most vigorously emphasized by Augustine in the passages we have cited.

A reason for unshakable faith is to be found in the presence of Christ who commissions his minister and works in him. Truth and grace are unfailingly present in the one who, in his name, imparts teaching and administers the sacraments, whatever be the personal holiness of that minister or his individual ability.

In his readiness to believe and obey those to whom has been entrusted the mission of doctors and pastors in the Church, the Christian knows that his faith and his obedience are really directed in the last analysis to Christ himself. There is nothing degrading or humiliating in the Christian's bowing before a person who is, in the first instance, like himself a fellow disciple of Christ and fellow member of Christ's flock, and who only teaches and governs in the name of Christ. For the priest, too, this certainty is the ground of an invincible hope, for he knows that he is relying, for the efficacy of his words and his action, upon him who alone gives life to the seed that men have planted and watered.

If all his trust is fixed on Christ, the priest cannot attribute anything to himself, nor can he tolerate others forgetting Christ to make the human minister the object of their esteem, their gratitude, and their affection. Even the bishop has no certain knowledge of how he appears in the eyes of God; still less can he presume upon his holiness for the future. "Here I speak to you as a bishop, in our Lord's name: what sort of person I am I do not know: how much less do you? For I can understand in some way what up to now I have been, but as to what I shall be at some later date, is there any way I can know that" (Sermon 340A, 8)?

Augustine's vision of the priesthood hits at the very roots of that "personality cult" that too often warps people's minds even in the Church, compromising the effectiveness of the priestly ministry, subordinating the higher interests of souls and of Christ himself to a mistaken regard for persons, encouraging silent complicity and servile adulation motivated by self-interest. "We are in greater danger," says Augustine, "from those who obey than from those who curse us; for the obedience of those beneath us rouses our pride, their curses exercise our patience" (Sermon 340A, 8).

It will be a good thing to recall, in this connection, a truth that Augustine never tires of emphasizing: the unity of the people of God, the "true equality" that reigns among all baptized Christians "in respect of the common dignity and action of all the faithful in building up the body of Christ," even granting the "distinction established by the Lord between the ministers of the altar and the rest of the people of God." The Constitution *Lumen gentium* (4, 32) cites in illustration of this assertion a passage of a sermon delivered by Saint Augustine on the anniversary of his own episcopal consecration: "My position at your head frightens me, but the condition I share with you consoles me. For you I am a bishop, with you I am a Christian. The first is the name of the office I have undertaken,[5] the second of grace: the first of danger, the second of salvation" (Sermon 340, 1). And elsewhere: "We, whom the Lord in his good pleasure and not for our own merit has set in this position, so dangerous on judgment day, have two distinct functions: one is to be Christian, the other is to be overseers (*praepositi*). Christians we are for ourselves, overseers for you" (Sermon 46, 2).

The bishop is "a fellow laborer" (*cooperarius*) with the faithful in the Lord's vineyard (Sermon 49, 2); like them and together with them, he is a fellow servant (*conservus*) (Sermon 229E, 2). "There is but one Lord, who has transformed us from servants into brothers and sisters, by redeeming us with his blood" (Sermon 260D, 2).

"For you we are as shepherds, but under that Good Shepherd we are sheep together with you. In this, our office, we are for you as masters, but under that one Master, in this school we are your fellow disciples" (*Expositions on the Psalms* 126, 3, 46). "What I have said I have learned from

---

5.   The Constitution has simply *nomen officii*, not *nomen suscepti officii* as in Saint Augustine and in Saint Caesarius of Arles.

him; and you, too, have surely learned it with me in this school. As preachers, we preside from a master's pulpit, but in the one and only school we have a common master in heaven" (Sermon 218, 5).

Similarly in that sermon already mentioned, in which the Bishop of Hippo speaks of the mission of a bishop on the occasion of an episcopal consecration: "To be worthy of his name (that is, bishop), let him listen not to me but with me. Let us listen together, and as fellow pupils in one school let us learn together from the one master, Christ, whose chair is in heaven, because his cross was first on earth" (Sermon 340A, 4).

Far from expecting praise, rarely sincere and almost always motivated by self-interest, the priest will rather ask of the faithful the aid of their prayers and of their loyal and industrious obedience. Augustine brings out this point and his thought will be reiterated and further developed by Saint Caesarius of Arles:

> In this great and so many-sided and varying office with its different concerns you must help us with your prayers and your obedience, so that we may delight not so much in being set over you as in being useful to you. For just as it is to your advantage that we should pray devoutly for God to be merciful to you for your salvation, so you too ought to pray to the Lord for us. . . . Just as we must reflect with great fear and anxiety on how we may fulfill the office of bishop without blame, so your own care must be to strive to be humbly obedient to all the commands given to you (Sermon 340, 1-2).

Augustine's vision of the priesthood therefore in no way imperils the dignity or the authority of that priesthood. On the contrary, the priesthood is ennobled and exalted (albeit within the limits of a theology of the priesthood that needed further deepening and development),[6] to a degree calculated to kindle the enthusiasm of all those honored with the mark of this office

---

6. See Pintard's reference to "open questions" in the conclusion of his *op. cit.*, pages 393-396.

and to inspire the deepest reverence and supernatural trust in the faithful. And the reason is not far to seek. It lies in Augustine's stress on the Christocentric nature of the priest-hood; its origin lies in a divine election. It power comes from the action of Christ himself, whose instrument it is, and its ideal is the service of fellow Christians for the love of Christ.

Ordination of Augustine as bishop. Ottaviano Nelli (1375-1444/50), Church of Saint Augustine, Gubbio, Italy.

8

The True Priest

SAINT AUGUSTINE NEVER WROTE a treatise on the priesthood as such. But his thinking on the office, responsibility, and duties of the priest, and more specifically of the bishop who embodies the fullness of the priesthood, finds abundant and quite detailed expression in many of his writings, especially his sermons to the faithful. Certain occasions in the life and activity of the bishop quite naturally give rise to such considerations. The annual celebration of the anniversary of his own episcopal consecration offers an ideal opportunity for an examination of conscience on the part of the bishop and for a reminder to his flock of their duty to respond to the loving care of their shepherd; the occasion of the consecration of a new bishop provides the perfect context for an explanation of the inner significance of this rite to the larger than usual congregation assembled for this solemnity; the commentary on certain scriptural texts leads naturally to reflections and exhortations on the subject of the priesthood; and on still other occasions, Augustine deliberately launches into this subject because of its importance in the life of the bishop and of the faithful.

HOLINESS OF THE TRUE PRIEST

It should be obvious to anyone who considers the very nature of the priesthood and the teaching of the scriptures on this noble and responsible office that any treatment of the priestly ministry must pay special attention to the holiness demanded by such an office and the virtue that should adorn any person bearing such a heavy responsibility. Yet it is not superfluous to remark on Augustine's quite special devotion to and insistence upon holiness as an integral part of the priestly mission. For Augustine is outstanding and unique among Christians, indeed among human beings, in his trenchant and implacable demand for veracity, a demand that tolerates neither exceptions nor limitations. In his own speculative endeavors, he is untiring in his search for the perfect reply that will assuage his thirst for truth, which is, at an even deeper level, the thirst for God. Likewise in the practical order, he would be incapable of making his peace with any attitude that did not correspond perfectly to the obligation assumed in the acceptance of a mission.

It is simply unthinkable that we could find in Saint Augustine any conception of the priesthood in which the features of authority, prestige, and personal interest in any form would be so predominant as to overshadow the demand for a total dedication to the office itself. Such a conception would be in flagrant conflict with the vision of the priesthood that emerges from holy scripture and from the most genuine tradition of the spiritual life. A rereading of Augustine's many depictions of the priesthood as a "service" will suffice to make this point crystal-clear.

It will be profitable at this point to recall a passage from a sermon preached by Augustine in 412 to the faithful of Carthage assembled to assist at the consecration of a new bishop. This sermon had three main aims, according to Augustine: that of reminding himself of his own duties, that of exhorting the new bishop, and that of instructing the faithful (Sermon 340A, 1); and the sermon is no less forceful and effective for being deliberately cast in the mold of popular rhetoric.

It is absolutely essential for the bishop, insists Augustine the preacher, to live up to his name.

> That is the sort of person a good bishop ought to be: otherwise he is no bishop. What use is it to an unfortunate man if his name happens to be lucky? If you saw a miserable

beggar whose name was Lucky, and addressed him by his name, saying, Come here, Lucky, go there, Lucky, get up, Lucky, sit down, Lucky, despite this name he would continue to be unfortunate. Something similar happens when you address a man as bishop, who is not a bishop at heart. What does the honor of the name bring him, except a heap of reproach? (Sermon 340A, 4).

In a completely different context, the demand for genuineness incumbent upon the priest is trenchantly affirmed by Augustine in his polemic against the Donatists. These latter had, as we have seen, insisted that the holiness of the minister was a necessary condition for the validity of the sacrament administered by that minister. Augustine is quick to refute that mistaken notion, but in the very refutation itself he readily admits that only the "righteous" priest has a true claim to the name of priest.

Petilian, a Donatist bishop, had objected: "If a man knows the priestly formulae by heart, is he indeed a priest simply because he proclaims these priestly formulae with a sacrilegious mouth?" In his reply, Augustine specifies that the subject of the discussion is the baptism administered, not the priest administering. However, he goes on to remark on the score of the priest:

> For a man to be a true priest (*verus sacerdos*), he must be clothed not only with the sacrament but also with righteousness, as it is written: *Your priests clothe themselves in righteousness* (Psalm 132:9). But the man who is a priest only in virtue of the sacrament, like the high priest Caiaphas, persecutor of the one and most true Priest, although he be not true himself, what he dispenses is true if he gives not of his own but what is of God, even as it is said of Caiaphas: *He did not speak in his own person; it was as high priest that he made this prophecy* (John 11:51).

Thus, the unworthy minister does not cease for that reason to be a true minister, inasmuch as he gives something that is true (and thus valid) because it is of God, but such an unworthy priest does indeed lack that "truth" or "genuineness" which consists in a proper correspondence of his life to his office, and in this he is guilty. Augustine insists that a clear-cut distinction must always be made between the priest's errors which are his own and the truth which he possesses, not as his own, but as coming from God. This distinction does indeed give the faithful comforting reassurance in their employment of the necessary means to salvation, but at the same time it recalls insistently to the priest himself the grave duty incumbent upon him to establish a proper harmony between his office and his conduct (*Against the Letters of Petilian* 2, 30, 68-69).

In our treatment of Augustine's approach to the dual element, human and divine, as co-present in the priest, we have already emphasized the frankness and even insistence with which, in his sermons and letters, Augustine refers to and admits the presence of good and bad pastors within the Church. Indeed he considers this state of affairs a permanent historical reality. But this does not make him any the less outspoken and vigorous in reproaching the bad pastors with their responsibility and threatening them with divine punishments. He obviously holds that the sad reality of the situation, though it may be quite understandable in terms of human nature's inclination to sin and the forces of evil always operative in history, nevertheless does not serve to attentuate the demand for holiness incumbent upon the priest.

In the context of an explanation of Jesus' admonitions to his seventy-two disciples (Luke 10:2-6), Augustine explains the mission and duties of shepherds of souls and proposes to them the supreme model of holiness: "Let us pay attention to our Lord, who is a true example and help to us. Let us prove that he is a help: *Without me you can do nothing* (John 15:5). Let us prove that he is an example: *Christ suffered for us,* Peter says, *leaving us an example, so that we should follow in his steps* (1 Peter 2:21)" (Sermon 101, 6).

Everything Augustine will have to say about priestly holiness will be simply a further development of the principles we have already learned from him in the preceding statements, for it will be simply the concrete demonstration of the real significance of the demand for veracity and genuineness incumbent upon the man and the Christian within the framework of the priestly mission.

THE HUMILITY OF THE PRIEST

It is not difficult to pinpoint the concrete form of holiness demanded of the priest who desires to substantiate by his life the name he bears in virtue of his office. We have but to look at the Augustinian conception of the priesthood as a "service" which we have already presented in Chapter 4. As for every Christian, so too for the priest, the essential duty is Christian love, which is proposed to the priest as a supreme ideal having its special claims upon him and involving in his case special demands for dedication and sacrifice. Yet we may be proceeding more in line with the spirit of Augustine if we begin with humility, the virtue he considers to be the foundation of the Christian life[1] and to rank as notably important in the context of priestly holiness.

An essential and primary mission of the priest is the ministry of preaching, as we have already seen in Chapters 5 and 6. And an indispensable condition of the proper preaching of Christ is humility. Augustine deduces this statement from the relation between the true and supreme shepherd, Christ himself, and those shepherds who represent him in his Church. Commenting on Saint John's gospel (10:1-10), Augustine illustrates his point by the figure of Christ as the door to the sheepfold. To enter into the fold by the door, he says, means primarily to preach "the true Christ." The heretics do not enter by the door. But the mere preaching is not enough.

> You must know that the fold of Christ is the whole of the Catholic Church. Whoever desires to enter the fold, let him enter by the door, that is preach the true Christ. And let him not only preach the true Christ but also seek the glory of Christ and not his own. Many have, by seeking their own glory, scattered the flock of Christ instead of uniting. Christ is indeed the low door; whoever would enter by this door must lower himself if he wants to get in without bumping his head badly. Whoever does not lower himself but rather

---

1. See Michele Pellegrino, *Give What You Command,* Catholic Book Publishing Company, New York, 1975.

puffs himself up is presuming to climb in through a hole in the wall; but anyone trying that is climbing for a bad fall (*Homilies on the Gospel of John* 45, 5).

In another sermon, Augustine applies the same scriptural text in the same sense, after having drawn an admonition to humility for preachers from a verse of the psalm he is in the process of commenting on:

> *Proclaim among the nations his glory* (Psalm 96:3). *It is his glory* you are to proclaim among the nations: yes, his glory and not your own. O builders, proclaim worthily his glory among the nations. Should you desire to proclaim your own glory, you would fall, but if you proclaim his glory, you will be built up even as you yourselves truly build. Whosoever, therefore, would proclaim his own glory thereby shows he does not desire to be in this house and consequently does not sing the new song together with all the earth.

Here Augustine is hitting at the Donatists, and he goes on to assert that pride and hyprocrisy are the causes of the schism. But the words we have just cited are applicable to all preachers, as are the ones that come next:

> *I am the door; it is by me that a person enters.* Who are these that enter in by the door? Those who seek God's glory and not their own. Who enters in by the door? Whoever does what is written: *Proclaim worthily among the nations his glory,* says the Lord, *but whosoever climbs in some other way is a thief and a robber* (John 10:1-2). He who goes in by the door is humble; he who climbs in some other way is proud; therefore is the former said to go in and the latter to climb. But the former, on entering, is welcomed; the latter, by his climbing, is thrown headlong (*Expositions on the Psalms* 95, 3).

Again in the following passage, the figure of Christ the door is interpreted as a warning to imitate the humility of the Savior as manifested in his incarnation and passion. Although Augustine does not here address himself explicitly to shepherds of souls, the entire context of the sermon makes it plain that they are foremost in his mind.

> You heard when the gospel was read to you, *He who enters by the door is the shepherd, but he who climbs in by another way is a thief and robber; he seeks to rout, scatter,*

and destroy (John 10:1-2.10). Who is it who enters by the door: One who enters through Christ. Who is such a person? One who imitates Christ's passion, who acknowledges Christ's humility, so that, since God was made human for us, we must acknowledge that we are not God but human. For those who, though they are human, wish to appear to be God, do not imitate him who, though he was God, was made human (Sermon 137, 4).

Later on in this same sermon, the Donatists are branded as the thieves that climb in by another way rather than entering by way of Christ. Their defect is pride, pride in attributing to themselves the power to sanctify and to justify (Sermon 137, 12).

The candid humility that ought to inspire the shepherd of souls finds one of its most compact and effective expressions in that play of words between *praeesse* and *prodesse* which was a favorite of Saint Augustine and which we reported in our treatment of his vision of the priesthood as service. It was Augustine's own motto and slogan, as he declares to the proconsul Hapringius, telling that official that the bishop of Hippo's concern and solicitude is directed entirely "to the Church entrusted to me, which I serve by making myself useful to that Church, desiring not so much to be at its head as to be at its side."

Augustine began his already mentioned sermon on the occasion of the consecration of a new bishop with a forthright and explicit admonition concerning the humility demanded of a bishop, who is the servant of the multitude, even as the Lord of lords willed to be a servant. Augustine recalls the apostles' dispute among themselves, motivated by the lust for power and status, and Christ's trenchant dissipation of the acrid fumes of their pride by his proclamation of the duty and necessity of becoming as humble as little children. He recalls likewise Saint Paul's warning against consecrating a neophyte bishop for fear that it might make him conceited; and Augustine declares that such warnings apply, in the first instance, to himself. He notes that Christ gave a stern lesson in humility, by word and, even before that, by example, to the sons of Zebedee with their status-seeking (Sermon 340A, 1-5). The whole of the first part of the sermon is devoted to showing how humility is an essential virtue of a bishop.

In the very name of the episcopal office, as he sees it mentioned in Saint Paul, Augustine discerns a call to humility. To say "bishop" (at least in the Latin-Greek context where *episcopus* at once conjures up overtones of overseer) is not to pronounce an honorary title but rather to define a laborious activity entirely devoted to the good of the Church, an activity calling for absolute unselfishness in its execution. Says the Apostle: "*He who aspires to the episcopate, aspires to a good work* (1 Timothy 3:1). He wanted to explain what sort of thing the episcopate is: a work, not an honorary position. . . . It is obvious that no man would be a bishop whose chief delight was to be at the head of people than at their side (*qui praeesse dilexerit, non prodesse)" (City of God* 19, 19).

We have already had occasion to recall the forthright tribute paid by Augustine to those bishops who, motivated by a deep sense of responsibility, renounced the episcopate when they became aware of shortcomings in themselves that rendered them less than fit for the fulfillment of their duties. It will be to the point here to emphasize Augustine's praise precisely for their humility: "certain men endowed with holy humility" (*Answer to Cresconius* 2, 11, 13).

COMMON CHRISTIAN CALLING

The feeling of sincere humility that ought to fill the mind and heart of the priest takes on a note of unusual concreteness and liveliness in the frequent passages in which Augustine is insisting on the fundamental equality between bishop and faithful in respect of the common Christian calling, without prejudice to the pastoral responsibility.

The parable of the laborers in the vineyard (Matthew 20:1-16) convinces Augustine that he is a fellow worker with his faithful fellow Christians in the Lord's vineyard:

Am I, by any chance, the one who has hired day laborers for the vineyard, I who cannot see into the heart? No, I am not the one who hires you by the day, who sends you to your work, who gets ready your wages. I am your fellow laborer; I labor in the vineyard with the powers he deigns to give me, and the spirit in which I labor, that he sees who has hired me by the day (Sermon 49, 2).

The fellow laborer is a fellow servant of the one true Master, as the same parable suggests:

Who are we? His ministers, his servants. What we bestow on you is not our own; we draw it from his storeroom. We ourselves live on it, for we are fellow servants (Sermon 49, 2).

We have a common Master; we portion out the food to our fellow servants; from this granary we too draw our own sustenance. We belong not to ourselves but to him who has shed his blood for our ransom. Together we have been ransomed; one and the same is the price of all. Our provender is the holy gospel. From servants he has made us brothers and sisters, he who ransomed us: the only-begotten Son has made us co-heirs (Sermon 260D, 2).

We are your servants: your servants, but also your fellow servants. We are your servants, but all of us have one Lord. We are your servants, but in Jesus, as the Apostle says: *But we are your servants through Jesus* (2 Corinthians 4:5). We have been placed at the head, and we are servants; we are in command, but only if we are useful (Sermon 340A, 3).

And he goes to explain that the bishop is a servant in the sense in which Christ is a servant and minister.

The same teaching is suggested by the parable of the Good Samaritan.

The robbers have left you half dead on the road, but you have been found by the Good Samaritan who was passing by; you have had wine and oil poured upon you, you have received the sacrament of the Only-Begotten; you have been set upon his own mount, you have believed in Christ incarnate; you have been brought to the inn, you are in the care of the Church. That is why I am speaking. And what I do, we all do: our position is that of innkeeper. To that innkeeper it was said: *I will pay you back whatever more you spend, when I come through here on my return* (Luke

10:35). If only we were at least spending our own earnings. But everything that we are expending, brethren, is the Lord's coin. We are your fellow servants; we, too, live from what serves to nourish the rest.

And the sermon concludes with an exhortation to humility and love for Christ and for neighbor:

Let no one attribute to us the good that he or she receives. We are wicked servants if we do not give it, and if we do give it, then we still cannot boast about that, seeing that we are not giving of our own. Let us all love him with all our heart; for him and through him and in him let us be united ourselves! We all have but one King; may we all succeed in reaching the one kingdom (Sermon 179A, 7-8).

Augustine sees the same inner meaning in two other gospel figures, that of the master and disciples, and that of the shepherd and the sheep. Himself a true and genuine shepherd, the bishop is, together with the faithful, a member of Christ's flock; himself a true and genuine master, he is yet their fellow disciple: "For you we are as shepherds, but under that Good Shepherd we are sheep together with you. In this, our office, we are for you as masters; but under that One Master, in this school we are your fellow disciples" (*Expositions on the Psalms* 126, 3). And a little earlier in the same sermon, Augustine has explained how such considerations serve as an incitement to humility: "It is a perilous business, that account that we must render of this high position, if we do not place ourselves, with all our heart, so as to be under your feet, if we do not pray for you, that he who knows your souls may guard you."

"We provide our fellow servant with the Lord's food; we feed the sheep in our Lord's pastures, and are fed with them" (*Homilies on the Gospel of John* 46, 8). In the one flock, under the staff of Christ the shepherd, "the shepherds, too, are sheep themselves" (*Homilies on the Gospel of John* 123, 5).

In a sermon on Saints Peter and Paul, having recalled that his own merits are gifts of God, Augustine concludes thus: "What I have said I have learned from him; and you, too, have surely learned with me in this school. As preachers, we preside from a master's pulpit, but in the one and only school we have a common master in heaven" (Sermon 218, 5).

Again, in another sermon on the feast of the same two saints, Augustine tells the faithful: "We feed you and we are ourselves fed together with you (*pascimus vos, pascimur vobiscum*). You are sheep of his flock and we together with you, for we are Christians. As I have said already: we feed you and we are ourselves fed together with you" (Sermon 296, 5. 13).

Christians like all the faithful, yet chiefs and leaders for the good of the faithful, the bishops cannot but feel the weight of the responsibility resting on their shoulders.

> We whom the Lord in his good pleasure and not for our own merit has set in this position, so dangerous on judgment day, have two distinct functions: one is to be Christians, the other is to be overseers (*praepositi*). Christians we are for ourselves, overseers for you. Being Christians is to our own advantage; being overseers is exclusively for your benefit. There are many Christians, not overseers, whose road to God is perhaps easier and who travel perhaps all the more quickly the lighter the burden they carry. We, on the other hand, besides Christians, on account of which shall have to render an account to God of our life, are also overseers, and therefore shall have to render an account to God of our ministry as well (Sermon 46, 2).

And Augustine reiterates this thought at the beginning of his next sermon (Sermon 47, 2).

The lesson of humility to be derived from such considerations is explicitly recalled in a sermon already several times cited, with this admonition addressed by Augustine to the new bishop:

> To be worthy of his name, let him listen not to me but with me; let us listen together, and as fellow pupils in one school let us learn together from the one master, Christ, whose chair is in heaven, because his cross was first on earth. He has taught us the way of humility: descending to ascend, visiting those who lay in the lowest depths, and raising those who wanted to be united to him (Sermon 340A, 4).

This sense of concreteness and immediate contact with his hearers, which we have mentioned above, finds a singularly lively expression in a sermon delivered by Augustine in the early years of his episcopate. Here the bishop not only puts himself on the same footing as his hearers, as a servant together with them of the one and only Lord; he even draws a lesson in modesty from the thought that there may well be among this listening congregation one who will himself be a bishop one day. Augustine here speaks in a tone of good-natured raillery and teasing insistence but that in no way derogates from the simple and forthright humility that prompts his words. He had just begun to speak of the duties of the bishop after having dealt with the duties of the rank and file of the faithful. Then he gets the idea (or perhaps the attitude of no small number of his congregation gives him to understand) that the congregation would gladly dispense with reflections that seem to have nothing to do with themselves:

> I have told you, then, what concerns you, but I want to tell you what is our own concern. But it may seem to some of you that I am bent on telling you something superfluous, and you may be thinking to yourselves: If only he would let us go now! He has already told us what concerns ourselves, but as for what concerns him, what is that to us? I think it is better that we should be of concern to you in our love of each other. You indeed belong to one household now, all of us who are stewards belong to the same household, and we all belong to one Lord. . . . And so you must listen to what concerns the steward, whether to congratulate each other, if you find any such among yourselves, or certainly to be instructed in the matter. For how many in this congregation are destined to be stewards? We too once stood where you are standing; we too, who are now seen distributing food to our fellow servants from a position above them, a few years ago were receiving food with our fellow servants down where you are. I speak as a bishop to the laity, but how do I know how many future bishops I am speaking to (Sermon 101, 4)?

Such reflections go to show how firmly rooted in Augustine's mind and heart is the sense of humility that inspires him in his mission as shepherd of souls. And it should be borne in mind that, in this, as in all his attitudes and feelings, his supreme norm is the example of Christ himself. He has said that the bishop is at once commander (*praepositus*) and serviceman, overseer and servant:

> Let us see, then, in what way the bishop who is put in command is a servant. In the same way as our Lord himself. For when he said to his apostles, *Whoever wants to be greatest among you must be your servant* (Matthew 20:26), for fear that human pride might take offense at the name of servant, he quickly consoled them, and by giving himself as an example encouraged them to do what he had commanded. *Whoever wants to be greatest among you must be your servant.* But observe how: *As the Son of man came not to be served but to serve* (Matthew 20:28 — Sermon 77A, 3).

GLOW WITH CHRISTIAN LOVE

Bishop Honoratus of Thiabe had asked Augustine what should be the stand of the various members of the clergy in the face of the barbarian invasions then sweeping over Africa: should they stay at their post and face all the risks involved in so doing? Or should they flee to help out the refugee Christians, or to hold themselves in readiness to exercise their ministry in new conditions? Augustine replied in the lengthy Letter 128. This letter, written near the end of his life, can well be considered as a kind of summary, left by the seventy-five year old bishop to the ministers of the Church, of all the pastoral teachings he had so generously imparted to them on countless occasions, as we have already had an opportunity of seeing.

This letter is pervaded with the wisdom gained from long study and diligent meditation of scripture and from an equally long and varied experience in the pastoral ministry. Augustine is here sharing his own reflections and convictions with a fellow bishop in a moment fraught with unusual difficulties and dangers for the very life of the Church, as it faces a grave and urgent problem. On the one hand there is the question of whether the ministers of the altar should risk their own lives or seek safety for the moment in order to preserve their usefulness for more propitious times and circumstances; on the other hand there is the problem of the spiritual needs of a whole people, who need the ministrations of the Church more than ever in such times of upheaval.

Without here going into details of this Augustinian reply, we would yet wish to emphasize one dominant thought that inspires the whole letter and suggests the line that concrete and individual solutions must take: Christian love is the essential virtue of anyone who has vowed himself to the service of the Church. We here limit ourselves to noting those passages of the letter in which this Christian love is explicitly mentioned. There are many other passages where that love is implicitly propounded, without being mentioned by name.

In the brief introduction, Augustine speaks of "the bonds of our ministry, wherewith the love of Christ has bound us" (section 1). The ministers of the altar who could have fled and chose rather to stay behind with their brothers and sisters exposed to danger have given the supreme proof of that Christian love extolled by Saint John when he says: *As Christ has laid down his life for us, so too ought we to lay down our lives for the brethren* (1 John 3:16 — section 3).

Thus, whoever stays behind in order not to abandon the ministry of Christ "is accomplishing a more generous work of charity than the man who flees, thinking not of his brothers and sisters but of himself, and who later, when captured, endures martyrdom rather than deny Christ" (section 4).

It would be hard to find any higher praise of pastoral Christian love than this of Augustine which declares it to be superior to martyrdom itself, when that martyrdom is not motivated by such Christian love.

Augustine readily admits that mortals can easily experience a sense of fear in the face of deadly danger. But they must put down that fear, strong in the power of the Lord. And this is possible "where the supernatural love of God is brightly burning and the worldly passions are not smoldering. This love says: *Do you think anyone is weak without my feeling his weakness? Does anyone have his faith upset without my longing to restore him* (2 Corinthians 11:29)? But this sort of love comes from God. Let us then pray that he will grant it to us who requires it of us" (section 7).

The case may, of course, arise in which some of the faithful remain in their homes to await the coming of the barbarians while others flee before the invading hordes; in such a case, some of the ministers of God must likewise remain and some must flee together with the fleeing Christians. Augustine expresses the hope that there will be a fraternal competition among the clergy to divide these assignments among themselves, with no one taking the slightest thought for his own personal advantage: "And such competition there will certainly be when all glow with Christian love and when all are pleasing to love himself, that is to God who is love" (1 John 4:8-16 — section 12).

In conclusion, Augustine once again refers to the two criteria that have dictated his reply: "truth," that is, loyalty to the norms indicated by the word of God, many times cited in the letter; and "Christian love," the supreme standard for the conduct of the ministers of God (section 14).

On the basis of the letter we have just been examining it is easy to stress the twin demand of Christian love levied on the minister of God, a twin demand to which Augustine refers in many other passages of his writings and sermons.

The first aspect of these twin demands is a negative one, and Augustine likes to refer to Pauline texts to articulate it. We find his favorite texts all assembled together in this very letter (section 9). Having recalled the good accruing to Christians from the presence of the ministers of Christ, he goes on:

> On the other hand, you see the damage done by their absence, when they are seeking their own interests and not those of Jesus Christ (Philippians 2:21), when they are lacking in that virtue of which it is said that it *does not seek its own* (1 Corinthians 13:5), when they are failing to imitate that great Apostle who said: *not considering my own advantage but their advantage, that if possible they may be saved* (1 Corinthians 10:33).

The first of the texts here cited is recalled by Augustine at the beginning of the long sermon on pastors. Commenting on Ezekiel 34, Augustine says: "This is the first reproach made to such pastors: that they feed themselves and not the flock.

Who are the pastors that feed themselves and not the flock? Those of whom the Apostle says: *All seek their own interests and not those of Jesus Christ*" (Sermon 46, 1). Those who take the preaching of the gospel in the Church as a pretext for seeking their own interests (money, honor, plaudits) are hirelings and not shepherds (Sermon 137, 5).

Augustine devolops this thought in his commentary on Christ's own distinction between true shepherds and hirelings. Here is an excerpt of that development:

> In the Church there are certain people in positions of authority, of whom the apostle Paul says: *They seek their own ends, not those of Jesus Christ.* What does it mean: *they seek their own ends*? They do not love Christ for nothing, they do not seek God for the sake of God; they pursue worldly rewards, their eyes are fixed on gain, and they long to be honored by their fellow creatures. When one in authority loves such things, and serves God for the sake of them, that is the sort of person who is a hireling, and not to be reckoned among the children of God (*Homilies on the Gospel of John* 46, 5).

Possidius knew Augustine through and through, and he stresses the zeal with which Augustine attended the many councils held in so many different and often distant provinces, "seeking in them not his own interests but those of Jesus Christ" (*Life* 21, 1).

Augustine is well aware that many of his own fellow priests and bishops are wicked shepherds and egotists deserving of Saint Paul's reproach. And he knows that there will always be such pastors within the Church; he reminds his correspondent Felicia of this sad fact of history to prevent her being shaken in her faith. After citing our Lord's own remark on scandals (Matthew 18:7), Augustine continues,

> Who are these men if not those of whom the Apostle says: *Who seek their own interests and not those of Jesus Christ*? There are therefore some men who use their pastoral office to look after Christ's flock, but there are others whose only thought, in that office, is for their own temporal honors and worldly advantage. Individuals of both sorts will come and go, but it is inevitable that these two types of pastors will always be present in the Catholic Church itself, right down

to the end of the world and Christ's last judgment (Letter 208, 2).

Paul, on the contrary, "did not seek his own interests but those of Jesus Christ" (Letter 208, 5). So do "the good shepherds that seek not their own interests but those of Jesus Christ" (Letter 208, 6).

The pastor who seeks his own interests is usurping the rights of Christ, treating Christ's flock as if it were his own, whereas that flock is the exclusive property of Christ himself:

> Note well, my brethren. Christ has said: *Feed* **my** *sheep, feed* **my** *lambs, feed* **my** *sheep* (John 21:15-17). **Mine,** he said, not **yours.** Feed, O good and faithful servant, the flock of the Lord marked with **his** sign. *Was it Paul who died on the cross for you? Were you baptized in the name of Peter and Paul* (1 Corinthians 1:13)? Well, then, feed **his** flock, washed in **his** baptism, signed with **his** name, ransomed with **his** blood. *Feed,* says Christ, **my** *sheep* (Sermon 295, 3; Sermon 196, 2; see Sermon 290, 3).
>
> Those who feed Christ's sheep with the desire to make them their own instead of Christ's are proved guilty of loving themselves and not Christ, by a passion for boasting, ruling, or acquiring possessions, instead of a love of obeying, helping, and pleasing God. So it is against those whom the Apostle laments over as seeking their own interests instead of those of Jesus Christ that these words of Christ, so insistently repeated, warn us. For what do the words mean: *Do you love me? Feed my sheep,* other than: If you love me, do not think it is you who feed them; but feed my sheep as mine, not your own; seek my glory in them, not your own; my rule, not your own; my profit, not your own. . . . Therefore let us love not ourselves but him; and in feeding his sheep seek his interests and not our own. . . . The vice which those who feed Christ's sheep have to guard against most of all is seeking their own interests instead of those of Jesus Christ, and using those for whom Christ's blood was shed to further their own ambitions (*Homilies on the Gospel of John* 123, 5).

You are sheep indeed, but you belong to him who has bought us and you. We have only one Master; he is a shepherd and no mere hireling. He feeds his sheep, and he has done more than is ever done for sheep; paid out the bond and drawn up the deed and testament. What is the price of that bond? His own most precious blood! What is the substance of that deed and testament? The gospel you have just been hearing. What did he say to Peter? *Do you love me? — Yes, Lord, I love you. — Feed my sheep. Mine,* remember, not *yours!* (Sermon 147A, 2).

It is true that Augustine explicitly attributes the presumption of appropriating the flock of Christ only to the heretics and the schismatics. But the principle he here enunciates is quite sufficient to restrain any tendency to self-love or self-seeking in anyone called to feed the flock that is not his own but the Lord's.

MAGNA CHARTA OF PRIESTLY LOVE

The Johannine passage just mentioned (John 21:15-17) is the *magna charta* of priestly love. And Augustine never wearies of showing that the thrice-repeated protestation of love that Jesus claimed from Peter before installing him as chief shepherd of his flock is of cardinal significance for the very mission being entrusted to Peter, since that mission is to be one long uninterrupted act of love for Christ the Master.

Christ's repeated questioning of Peter was aimed at Peter's own instruction, says Augustine, for

Christ could not be ignorant of Peter's inmost feelings. Three times the question is repeated and three times love replies: he who had thrice denied out of fear is thrice put to the question on love. . . . After a single, a double, a triple profession, the flock is committed to his charge. *Do you love me?* says the Lord. *Lord, you know that I love you!* replies Peter. And Christ: *Feed my lambs.* And this once, twice, thrice over; as if there were no other way for Peter to show his love for Christ except by being a faithful shepherd under the chief of all shepherds. *Do you love me? I love you!* What, then, will you give me, since you love me? What will you, man, give to me, your Creator? What thing will you produce from your love to offer it, you ransomed one, to your redeemer, you soldier, to your king? What will you offer me? One thing only do I require of you: *Feed my sheep!* (Sermon 147A, 1).

And this is but one of several instances in which Augustine comments on this gospel episode along these same lines (Sermon 137, 3-4; Sermon 245, 4; Sermon 229P).

It is this love of Christ that has made Peter himself a good shepherd, he who was appointed by Christ who said: *I am the Good Shepherd.*

> Let us question our Lord as intelligently as we can, and enter into discussion with the utmost humility, since we are speaking with so great a head of so great a household. What do you mean, Lord, you who are the good shepherd? For it is you, the good lamb, who tell us you are the good shepherd; you are the shepherd and also the pastures, the lamb and also the lion. What do you mean? We must listen, and you must help us to understand. *I,* you say, *am the Good Shepherd.* What was Peter? Was he not a shepherd, or was he a bad one? Let us see if he was not a shepherd. *Do you love me?* That was what you asked him, Lord, *Do you love me?* and he answered, *Yes, I love you.* And so you told him: *Feed my sheep.* You, you, Lord, by your question, and by the confirmation of your own words, made the one who loved you a shepherd. Therefore he, to whom you entrusted the feeding of your sheep, is a shepherd. He is a shepherd at your own recommendation. Now let us see whether he is not good. We can find out from that very question and his own answer. You asked him whether he loved you, and he answered. *Yes, I love you.* You saw into his heart, and saw his answer was true. Is he not good, then, for loving someone so good? . . . In saying he loved you, and speaking from his inmost heart, he answered truthfully. Moreover you have told us: *Good people speak good words from the good treasure house of their hearts* (Matthew 12:35). Therefore he was a shepherd of shepherds; yet even he was a shepherd, and was also good, and in the same way the rest were good shepherds (Sermon 138, 4).

It is precisely this honest love that leads the pastor to seek Christ and not himself in his ministry:

> The Lord questioned him, as you have heard in the reading of the gospel, and said to him: *Simon, son of John, do you love me more than these?* And Peter replied and said: *Yes, Lord, you know that I love you.* A second and third time did the Lord ask him the very same question. Peter replied that he loved Christ and Christ entrusted to Peter his flock.

Indeed every time that Peter replied: *I love you,* the Lord
Jesus would say: *Feed my lambs! Feed my sheep!* In the
person of Peter was prefigured the unity of all pastors, of all
pastors, that is, who are good shepherds and know how to
pasture and feed the flock of Christ for his sake and not for
their own (Sermon 147, 2).

Feed my sheep! Why? Because you love me sincerely, I
entrust to you my sheep: feed them, but forget not that they
are mine (Sermon 2290, 3).

Peter denied, Peter wept, and with his tears washed out
the stain of his denial. Christ rose again, Peter was put to the
question on love; he received the sheep entrusted to him not
as his own but as Christ's. For Christ had not said to him:
Feed your sheep but *Feed my sheep.* Feed those that I have
bought, for you too have I redeemed (Sermon 299B, 2).

Christ's triple interrogation of Peter is presented by Augustine in the passages just cited as a reminder of the triple denial
into which the Apostle had fallen. There is another reference
to this connection in Augustine's commentary on the gospel of
John: "The triple confession repays the triple denial, so that
the tongue may not serve love less than fear, and imminent
death seem to have evoked a greater response than present
life. Let it be the task of love to feed the Lord's flock, if it was
the mark of fear to deny the shepherd" (*Homilies on the
Gospel of John* 123, 5).

Christian love, especially in the pastor of souls, is that
conjugal purity of heart in which the bride loves the bride-
groom, God, for himself and not for any ulterior motive. The
apostle Paul

says that some preach the gospel for love, others for
opportunity, about whom he says, *they do not preach the
gospel rightly* (Philippians 1:17). The matter is right, but
they themselves are wrong. What they preach is right, but
the preachers are wrong. Why are they wrong? Because
they seek something else in the Church; they are not seeking
God. If they sought God, they would be chaste, for God is
the soul's legitimate husband. Whoever seeks something
from God other than God does not seek God chastely. You
see, my friends: if a wife loves her husband because he is
wealthy, she is not chaste. For rather than loving her
husband, she loves his money. But if she loves her husband,

she loves him even when he is poor, even when he has nothing. . . . So those who preach God because they love God, those who preach God, because of God, feed his sheep, and are not hirelings. It was the chastity of the soul that our Lord Jesus Christ demanded, when he said to Peter, *Peter, do you love me?* What does it mean, *Do you love me?* Are you chaste? Have you a heart that is not adulterous? Do you seek in the Church, not your own interests, but mine? If, then, you are such a person, and you love me, *feed my sheep.* For you will not be a hireling, but a shepherd (Sermon 137, 9-10).

PASTORAL CHRISTIAN LOVE

Pastoral Christian love is centered upon Christ. The triple interrogation of Peter by Christ himself clearly proclaims the pastor's supreme duty as that of loving Christ, and Augustine never tires of returning to this episode to point the pastor to the ideal that ought to inspire him his whole life through. But the mystical union between Christ and the faithful, between the shepherd and the flock, between the head and the members, is so fundamental to Augustine's theology and spirituality, that he finds it easy to make the transition from the love that binds the bishop to Christ to the love with which that same bishop loves the Church.

In his commentary on Psalm 45, 17: *Instead of your fathers, sons are born to you,* Augustine says that the apostles are the fathers who have engendered the Church. The bishops, their successors, are the sons the Church itself has engendered and established upon the throne and in the place of their fathers. They are her rulers and princes, "mindful of her name from generation to generation, that is until this age shall pass away after it runs the course of its many generations. They have charge and care" of the Church, "the bride of Christ, the Queen who is the King's daughter, to the end that, freed from this age, she may reign with God for all eternity" (*Expositions on the Psalms* 44, 32).

Christian love kindles the zeal of the pastor so that he does not recoil before labor and sacrifices. "If we have the shepherd

heart of the true pastor, we must bear our way through the
thorny hedges. We must seek the sheep, even to the laceration
of our own bodies, and we must bring it back with joy to the
shepherd and prince of all" (*Proceedings with Emeritus* 12).

The lost sheep may flee the shepherd who is looking for it,
but that will not make the shepherd desist from his efforts, for
he is impelled by the love of Christ. In such terms does
Augustine address himself to the Donatists: "We seek you
out, therefore, to find you. We desire that you should have life,
for we love you as much as we hate your error" (*Answer to the
Writings of Petilian* 1, 38, 89).

The conversation of the risen Christ with Peter does more
than simply proclaim, in the most forthright manner possible,
the supreme duty of pastoral Christian love. It also stresses the
fact that love must be unlimited, must impel the pastor even to
the sacrifice of his own life, if that be the will of God:

> The example he (Peter) has seen from the Lord himself in
> the flesh has made him strong, showing him that death is no
> more to be feared. Now he will learn to love; now he cannot
> but love; now that he has seen the Lord alive again after
> death, his love is sure and firm, for he knows he will follow
> that Lord of his. And so when the Lord says: *Peter, do you
> love me?* his answer is: *Yes, Lord, I love you!* And the Lord
> then intimates: I do not want you to die for me, now that you
> love me; that is what I have done already for you. But what
> is the manner of your love for me? What will your love-gift
> be to me? Do you love me? *Feed my sheep.* And a second
> time the question and the answer; and a third! Three times
> must love confess for three times had fear denied. Note it
> well, grasp its meaning, learn from it, this threefold en-
> counter. No other question does Christ pose but only this:
> "Do you love?" No other answer does Peter give but only
> this: "I love." And Christ's reponse to this reply is always
> the same: *Feed my sheep.* Having thus entrusted his flock to
> Peter and taken Peter together with the flock under his own
> pastoral care, Christ foretells to Peter what he shall suffer,
> saying: *When you were younger, you used to dress yourself
> and go where you liked, but when you are an old man, you
> are going to stretch out your hands and someone else will
> dress you and take you where you do not want to go. He
> said this,* the evangelist tells us, *to show the kind of death*

by which Peter was going to glorify God. You see how
feeding the flock of the Lord demands of a man that he
should not refuse to die for the Lord's flock.

Christ may ask so much of the shepherd of his sheep
because he has himself ransomed them at the price of his
own blood. *"Feed my sheep.* I entrust my sheep to you.
What sheep? The sheep I have bought with my own blood.
For them I died. Do you love me? Then die for them!" The
servant of a man appointed to such service by a mortal
master would indeed be expected to pay up for the sheep
that were destroyed. Peter shed his blood for the sheep.

What was said to Peter, continues Augustine, was said to
the other disciples as well; and even as Peter fulfilled the
commission entrusted to him, so did they all; and they have
handed on that same commission right down to us, the pastors
of today. "We feed you and we are fed with you. May the Lord
grant us the power to love you to the point of being able to die
for you either in fact or in feeling" (Sermon 296, 1).

The same thought is developed in Augustine's commentary
on Christ's words: *The Good Shepherd lays down his life for
his sheep.* Here too, Augustine recalls the question put to
Peter, that disciple's reply, and Jesus' prediction of Peter's
martyrdom. "This, then," he concludes, "is the meaning of the
words: *Feed my sheep:* you are to lay down your life for my
sheep" (*Homilies on the Gospel of John* 47, 2).

Augustine does not hesitate, in the sermon already several
times cited, to admonish the bishop who has just been
consecrated that this is his duty if he wishes to merit the name
of bishop.

Next, when our Lord had entrusted his sheep to him for the
third time, he told Peter, who in answering and acknowl-
edging his love had condemned and destroyed his fear:
*When you were young, you girded yourself and went where
you liked, but when you are old, another will gird you and
take you where you do not wish to go. He said this to
indicate by what death he would glorify God.* He foretold
to him that his own cross and his own passion would also be
his. Go that way, the Lord says, and *Feed my sheep:* suffer
for my sheep. That is the sort of person a good bishop ought
to be; otherwise he is no bishop (Sermon 340A, 3-4).

Augustine mirrors the attitude of the whole of the primitive Church in taking every opportunity to extol the strength and courage of the martyrs and hold them up to the faithful for imitation. But the charism of martyrdom is reserved to a few of the Lord's flock who are called to witness with their blood to their loyalty to him; as for the pastors of that flock, they must be ready and willing to fight to the death for the truth. This line of reasoning we find in Augustine's commentary on John 21, where Christ's injunction to Peter is interpreted as a program of action for all shepherds of souls, a program proposed and enjoined upon them by that same Christ who has gone before us to set us an example by his death which he suffered for our sakes. The love for Christ

> in those who feed his sheep, should grow to such great spiritual ardor as to conquer even the natural fear of death. . . . But whatever the trouble of death, the power of love must conquer it, the love with which he is loved who, since he is our life, was willing to endure even death for us. For if we had no trouble, not even a little, in dying, the glory of the martyrs would not be so great. But if the good shepherd, who laid down his life for his sheep, made so many of those sheep martyrs for himself, how much more must those to whom he entrusts the feeding of his sheep, that is, the teaching and guiding of them, fight to the death for truth and against sin? And therefore, with the example of his passion set before us, who cannot see that the shepherds must rather cling to the shepherd by following his example, if many of the sheep have also followed his example, and under which one shepherd in one flock even the shepherds themselves are sheep? He has indeed made all his sheep, for all of whom he died; for he too was made a sheep, so that he might die for all (*Homilies on the Gospel of John* 123, 5).

As we have already noted, in our treatment of Letter 228, the proof of Christian love demanded of the pastor in the face of the threat to his flock occasioned by the barbarian invasions may well oblige the pastor to lay down his own life. Augustine asserts this duty, basing himself on the words of John (1 John 3:16), to the effect that we must imitate Christ in laying down our life for the brethren (Letter 228, 3). And the spiritual death in sin of the members of Christ is more to be feared than any tortures that the enemies can inflict upon our bodies (Letter 228, 7).

This insistence on the shepherds of Christ's flock proving their pastoral love even to the extent of laying down their lives may seem excessive. It may seem that the real demands upon pastoral love in the concrete will rather take the form of the daily duties of the care of souls. But the supreme demand on every pastor so permeates the whole of Augustine's thought and utterances that any faithful presentation of that thought must find due place for it. Nor is the man who for forty years labored tirelessly in the see of Hippo (and beyond, much beyond) insensitive to the weight of the pastoral ministry as that weight makes itself felt in the nagging demands of every day. We have already had occasion to note how Augustine, like other bishops of his day, had to face a constant round of duties that were by no means always exclusively spiritual. These secular commitments often filled his whole day and wore him out (Letter 48, 1). To this was added, in Augustine's case, the commitment to the other churches of Africa and to the Church universal, and the continuous demands of those looking to his wisdom for the solution of doubts and the exposition of the Catholic doctrine on so many questions. The sacrifice involved was all the greater for a man so temperamentally attracted to the contemplative life, so desirous of probing into the subtle secrets of truth and of encountering God in the silence of meditation, worship, and hidden loving.

Augustine's whole life, from the day of his ordination to the priesthood, was devoted to the fulfillment of that program he would outline in his *City of God* (19, 19):

> The Christian love of truth seeks holy leisure; the obligation imposed by that Christian love shoulders the appropriate assignment. If no one imposes this burden, then we must apply ourselves to the understanding and contemplation of truth; if the burden is imposed upon us, then we must shoulder it in the name of the obligation of Christian love.

Augustine's reminder of the demands of a Christian love that can make a person even lay down his or her life, if need be, is a timely lesson for the clergy of our day, who are being so earnestly admonished on so many sides to a life of devotion and heroism, to a surmounting of any compromise between an easy worldly life and the spirit of the gospel. Reflection on Augustine's words, and, even more important, on the word of God which was their inspiration, cannot but serve as a salutary stimulus to the priest who intends to devote himself entirely to the realization of his ideal.[2] Certainly the priest can, like Peter, whom Augustine calls a "denier out of human weakness," give way to temptation. But if he will but listen to the voice of Christ, questioning him about love, entrusting to him, in the name of that love, those sheep for whom he has shed his own blood, predicting for him a death like his own, then as "a lover by God's grace" (Sermon 229P) it will not be long before the priest resumes his journey with renewed will and confidence.

---

2.   See *"We Are Your Servants," Augustine's Homilies on Ministry,* Augustinian Press, 1986, for an English translation of the following sermons: Homilies on the Gospel of John 46; Sermon 340A; Sermon 340; Sermon 339; Sermon 101; Homilies on the Gospel of John 123, 4-5; Sermon 46, 1-11; Sermon 94; Sermon 137; Sermon 138.